Dani Nabudere's Afrikology

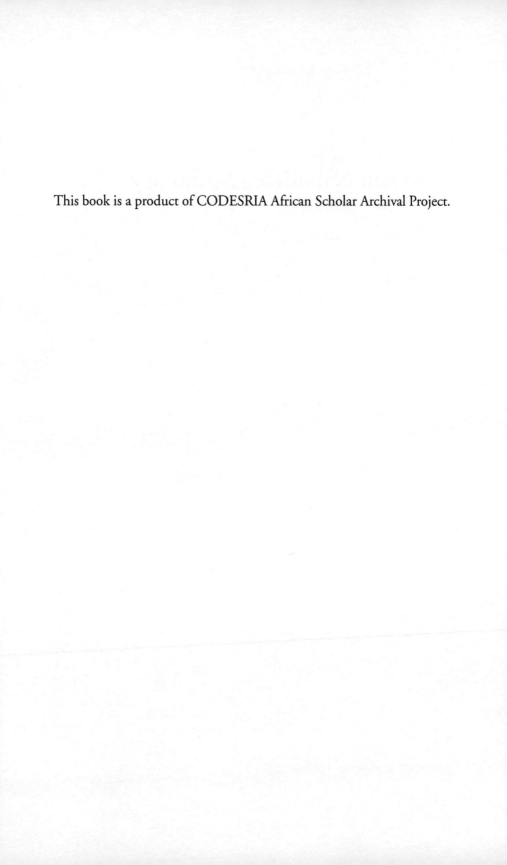

Dani Nabudere's Afrikology

A Quest for African Holism

Sanya Osha

CODESRIA

Council for the Development of Social Science Research in Africa
DAKAR

© CODESRIA 2018

Council for the Development of Social Science Research in Africa
Avenue Cheikh Anta Diop, Angle Canal IV
BP 3304 Dakar, 18524, Senegal
Website : www.codesria.org

ISBN: 978-2-86978-753-7

Typesetting: Alpha Ousmane Dia

Distributed in Africa by CODESRIA
Distributed elsewhere by African Books Collective, Oxford, UK
Website: www.africanbookscollective.com

The Council for the Development of Social Science Research in Africa (CODESRIA) is an independent organisation whose principal objectives are to facilitate research, promote research-based publishing and create multiple forums geared towards the exchange of views and information among African researchers. All these are aimed at reducing the fragmentation of research in the continent through the creation of thematic research networks that cut across linguistic and regional boundaries.

CODESRIA publishes *Africa Development*, the longest standing Africa based social science journal; *Afrika Zamani*, a journal of history; the *African Sociological Review*; the *African Journal of International Affairs*; *Africa Review of Books* and the *Journal of Higher Education in Africa*. The Council also co-publishes the *Africa Media Review*; *Identity, Culture and Politics: An Afro-Asian Dialogue*; *The African Anthropologist, Journal of African Tranformation, Method(e)s: African Review of Social Sciences Methodology*, and the *Afro-Arab Selections for Social Sciences*. The results of its research and other activities are also disseminated through its Working Paper Series, Green Book Series, Monograph Series, Book Series, Policy Briefs and the CODESRIA Bulletin. Select CODESRIA publications are also accessible online at www.codesria.org.

CODESRIA would like to express its gratitude to the Swedish International Development Cooperation Agency (SIDA), the Carnegie Corporation of New York (CCNY), the Norwegian Agency for Development Cooperation (NORAD), the Rockefeller Foundation, the Open Society Foundations (OSFs), The Open Society Initiative for West Africa (OSIWA), The Open Society Initiative for Southern Africa (OSISA), Andrew Mellon Foundation, and the Government of Senegal for supporting its research, training and publication programmes.

Contents

Preface

Dani Wadada Nabudere, the illustrious Ugandan scholar who passed away in 2011, produced a diverse body of work on various aspects of African culture, politics, and philosophy. Toward the end of his life, he formulated a theoretical construct that he termed "Afrikology." Unlike most other Afrocentrists, who have stopped with the task of proving the primacy of the Egyptian past and its numerous cultural and scientific achievements, Nabudere strenuously attempts to connect that illustrious heritage with the African present. This, remarkably, is what makes his project worthy of careful attention.

Essentially, Nabudere's philosophy of Afrikology traces the historical, cultural, scientific, and social links between the "Cradle of Humankind" and the contemporary world, with a view to healing the seismic severances occasioned by violence, false thinking, war, loss, and dispossession in order to accomplish an epistemological and psychic sense of wholeness for an African collective self. Before then, he worked extensively on different issues in African politics, most especially his trenchant critiques of imperialism. Now is a suitable time to begin to critically examine his various intellectual formulations with a view to situating his work properly within the apposite traditions of African scholarship.

This study takes on the urgently required task of evaluating Nabudere's location and contributions as an eminent African scholar. First of all, his formulations on politics and African philosophy are examined. This work also juxtaposes his corpus with primarily those of Cheikh Anta Diop and Molefi Kete Asante, whose corpora in many ways influence and intersect with Nabudere's work, in order to isolate recurrent trends in contemporary Africana thought and the influence of their legacies. This aspect of the project, hopefully, seeks to deepen the theoretical range of the book. In other words, it brings Nabudere's work into conversation with his Africanist peers to better underline his singularity as a thinker and theorist, even if he is one who, as this work will show, leaves much to be desired. Finally, the work of the Dutch anthropologist, Wim M. J. van Binsbergen is examined as it intersects with many of Nabudere's preoccupations.

It needs to be emphasized that this book is not merely a paean to Nabudere. Instead, it stands, hopefully, as a critical point of reference on his oeuvre. As such, this study provides a critical analysis of Nabudere's contributions to the broad field of African scholarship and of his stature in the discipline of African studies. His corpus is multidisciplinary, although a major preoccupation with Africa is discernible in virtually all his works. His writings deal with critiques of imperialism, African political systems, processes of globalization and Africa's location within them, and finally the ideological and existential imperatives of Afrocentric discourse. Toward the final segment of his career, he was solely preoccupied with Afrikology, which marks a major advance in his development as a conceptual thinker.

Finally, the study critiques the concept of Afrikology with a view to unearthing its full epistemological value. Before embarking on the concept, Nabudere's work on the African condition was characterized by a presentism that sometimes bordered on journalism. The exploration of Afrikology signified a transition to protohistory and hence, more proper academic discourse. Nonetheless, both approaches have their advantages. Presentism represents a populist immediacy, while Afrikology grants a degree of respectability and scholarly legitimacy. Protohistory, as it relates to Africa, is a more comforting discourse, since its distance prevents unwanted scrutiny. The distance also provides an opportunity for historical reinvention, which presentism cannot readily offer. As for theory, protohistory is also more amenable. Contemporary Africa can no longer blame its woes on colonialism and apartheid. It no longer has a blank canvas upon which to inscribe its failures that now appear to emanate directly from it. It has instead become a self-invented gargoyle that must speak for itself, unlike in the past when it allowed its foes to speak on its behalf. The present speaks in a myriad of unknown tongues, which is why it becomes difficult to find the connections between the past, what lies between, and the future. That is the level of responsibility involved in presentist analysis that, under protohistory, is not evident.

Nabudere's work prior to his elucidation of the concept of Afrikology can be characterized as an absence of theory or, at best, half-hearted forays in search of a theory. Africa, as we know, was the center of his concerns; i.e., Africa, in spite of its remarkable past, as victim of a brutal and persisting (post)colonial order. However, with the conceptualization of Afrikology, Nabudere finally came into his own; a voice discovered or, more appropriately, rekindled in the scalding ashes of postcolonial critique and the reoccurring realities of postcolonial malaise. But how forceful and original is his voice?

Nabudere quietly appropriated the projects of Afrocentricity such as those of Diop and Asante without due engagement with their particulars. So, rather than merely examining his voice in its isolated singularity, it is more representative to establish it within a discursive continuum to which both Diop and Asante belong. Nabudere's project is not original, even though, from an Afrocentric perspective, it is significant. But analytically, both its significance and failures can be interrogated when situated in an intellectual and historical context that addresses the same issues he seeks to problematize. Even if Nabudere's problematizations had not gone beyond those of the original Afrocentrists, it would still have been necessary to engage them as he often attempts to present his project as an isolated totality unconnected with other similar work or traditions. This approach ends up in a conceptual incongruity requiring urgent attention.

In addition to Diop and Asante, it is necessary to read Nabudere's work alongside the discourse of protohistory – hence the inclusion of Van Binsbergen's interventions. A central claim of Afrikology is that Africa is the Cradle of Humankind. This large claim requires substantiation with knowledge in the fields of comparative linguistics, comparative mythology, archaeology, anthropology, and genetics. Nabudere does not demonstrate the kind of awareness that fully addresses, or at least, incorporates this vital methodological imperative. Diop, on the other hand, is more aware of the significance of this methodological necessity and sets out to address it with the required seriousness.

Asante, to some degree, recognizes the importance of rigorous methodology in projects of Afrocentric intent. But his contributions to the discourse are of a different nature. The Atlantic slave trade had highly transformative and profound effects. It created new worlds, new beings, and new civilizations. What were supposed to be vast literal deathscapes ended up producing forms of life and creativity that attest to the ingenuity and creativity of the black race. Slavery was not meant to be regenerative in the ordinary sense of the word. It was meant, instead, to enforce a conception of work that divorced the worker (in this case, the slave) from it (work); it sought to implement a notion of work that signified utter sterility and spiritless abjection in which, by a paradoxical movement, it was able to produce death on a mass scale as its reoccurring signature. Asante understands the devastation wrought by slavery but more importantly, he comprehends that in its unremitting dynamic to establish sterility and regression as the black subjects' essential condition, it ended up transposing them into realms of unanticipated liberty. This liberation was not merely of the physical kind. In fact, this, at this stage, is less important, as the profundity of this liberation was the sort that enabled death to erupt with life, laughter, and song in a miracle of creation. Death, in effect, was compelled to birth precisely what it was not meant to; a freedom that liberated the slave beyond the reach and power of the slave master.

It seems impossible for Afrocentricity to compose itself without its mirror: Eurocentrism. Afrocentricity, just as other philosophies of blackness before it – négritude and African personality – requires its conceptual twin to breathe, and without which, it would appear difficult to sustain an independent existence of its own. Afrocentricity is aware of the numerous feints and deceptions of Eurocentrism because every time the demise of the latter and racism are proclaimed, a fresh assault is made upon the heart of former. Eurocentrism and Afrocentricity often act as conjoined twins with Eurocentrism serving as a dagger that shadows every move of its conceptual twin. But even more than this cloak and dagger relationship, Afrocentricity continually celebrates its freedom and remains resolutely close to the rhythms of joy and catharsis in contrast to the immensity, solitude, and relentlessness of the dialectic. The dialectic, totally devoid of spirituality, prefers the awful, comfortless reality of its devastation; infinity becomes far more terrifying than immortality: it becomes a nightmare for which there can never be some respite. Afrocentricity, having avoided this sterile, endlessly repetitive future, re-establishes a connection that collapses the distinction between heart and intellect even though it would forever remain an anomalous juxtaposition.

One of Afrocentricity's most remarkable hallmarks is its ability to wrest joy from the clutches of death and to identify how liberation is actually an opportunity to mourn. This goes against the tenets of conventional philosophy, which would rather endure as an activity that finds a reason to repeat itself ad nauseam. In other words, Afrocentricity refuses to be a philosophy of joylessness that, in the face of the overwhelming dominance of the dialectic constitutes an affront to philosophy, not within its centre but at its murky, disavowed margins. Afrocentricity sprang from death, a luscious experience of death, a death that demanded that its victims dance and sing as they yielded sacrificial offerings of blood, tears, and semen to it even as it still was not appeased. Afrocentricity rose from a gluttonous death and as a sign of triumph over it, Afrocentricity had to wrest laughter that continually rings from the bitterest parts of the heart. Otherwise, it would remain a perpetual, inconsolable slave to it (death). If the dialectic had become the sole momentum of philosophy, death had threatened to be Afrocentricity's permanent condition and feature. However, Afrocentricity has been able to effect a complete refusal of this proposition and hence philosophy's unyielding hostility toward it.

Furthermore, if Eurocentrism is Afrocentricity's conceptual twin, the relationship, curiously, is marked by a great distance, by a total lack of communication, in which the same conflicts between the two are endlessly rehashed without the ultimate confrontation that could lead to a resolution.

This work prepares the stage for a much-needed conversation across the meaningless conflicts that refuse to generate mutual understanding. The refusal or inability of Afrocentricity and Eurocentrism to understand each other is quite striking. This work is not primarily about effecting an alteration of this state of affairs – even as it provides what ought to be worthwhile source of contemplation – but an effort to engineer a juxtaposition that demonstrates why the misunderstandings occur so frequently. The misunderstandings stem from both Afrocentricity and Eurocentrism pursuing different aims and interests that are often unrelated even when they address similar concerns. Such aims and interests are never aligned to engender mutual understanding.

I thank Ebrima Sall, ex-Executive Director of the Council for the Development of Social Science Research in Africa (CODESRIA), for believing in this project from the outset, including the CODESRIA Documentation, Information, and Communication Centre (CODICE), under which it was executed. CODESRIA not only supported the project morally but also financially, which makes a huge difference between intention and realization. I thank my colleagues at the Department of Science and Technology-National Research Foundation of South Africa Centre of Excellence in Scientometrics and Science, Technology, and Innovation Policy (DST-NRF CoE STI), Institute for Economic Research on Innovation (IERI), and Tshwane University of Technology, Pretoria, namely Rasigan Maharajh and Mario Scerri, who have suported my work for many years. Finally, my gratitude goes to Elizabeth D. Boepple for her diligent editorial work.

The Author

Sanya Osha is a research fellow at the Department of Science and Technology – National Research Foundation of South Africa Centre of Excellence in Scientometrics and Science, Technology, and Innovation Policy (DST-NRF CoE STI) in the Institute for Economic Research in Innovation at Tshwane University of Technology, Pretoria, South Africa. He is also a fellow of the Africa Studies Centre, Leiden, the Netherlands. He is the author of *Kwasi Wiredu and Beyond: The Text, Writing and Thought in Africa* (2005), *Ken Saro-Wiwa's Shadow: Politics, Nationalism and the Ogoni Protest Movement* (2007), *Postethnophilosophy* (2011), and *African Postcolonial Modernity: Informal Subjectivities and the Democratic Consensus* (2014). He is also a co-editor of *The Africana World: Fragmentation to Unity and Renaissance* (2012) and editor of *The Social Contract in Africa* (2014).

1

A World War in Africa

Dani Wadada Nabudere (1980; 1994; 2003; 2004; 2006) produced a number of studies dealing with the political situation in the Democratic Republic of Congo (DRC) that evince his long-held ideological positions regarding the state and future of the African continent. Although in these studies, he does not develop a full-blown theory regarding the African condition, they indicate where his true interests and concerns lie. Also, employing the case of the DRC sociopolitical debacle as a point of departure, he is able deduce more general pronouncements about the entire continent. Through these studies, it is also possible to predict the development of his later ideas and concepts about the African situation.

Nabudere refers to the political crises in the DRC as Africa's "first world war." In a way, he has a point, in that the DRC has been transformed into a veritable theater of war involving a number of countries, interests, mercenaries, and a wide range of self-serving actors. As such, the fate of the DRC is no longer to be decided by its citizens and inhabitants alone, but by a perplexing assortment of countries, interests, and actors. The DRC is in a unique, if rather unfortunate, position of experiencing the effects of crippling internal combustion on the one hand, and the persistent onslaught of a formidable array of external forces on the other. Meanwhile, it has lost the capability to deal with these two (internal and external) fronts in a manner that ensures the resolution of the crises. Thus, Nabudere referring to the nexus of crises within the DRC as Africa's first world war becomes understandable.

This chapter examines Nabudere's monograph, *Africa's First World War: Mineral Wealth, Conflicts and War in the Great Lakes Region* (2004) as an introductory basis for his ideas on Africa and the specific theoretical turn they took within the general movement of his subsequent thought. Indeed, Africa and Afrocentric concerns have always been pronounced at the very beginning of his work.

Nabudere locates the beginnings of the DRC crises in the 1884–1885 Berlin Conference (under the presiding influence of Chancellor Otto von Bismarck), which led to the partitioning of African territories by the dominant European powers of the day. The Great Lakes Region of Africa was viewed by the foreign powers as a vital economic hub and hence the much-mentioned "scramble for Africa" occurred. Frantz Fanon employed the metaphor of a trigger to typify the Great Lakes Region (and the African continent in general) as being the reason for the European scramble. These series of Balkanization of the African geographical landscape, cultural and political realities had the combined effect of eventually causing the necessity for the recolonization of the continent in Nabudere's view. Apart from preempting a dire political future for the continent, the cultural and political Balkanization had the immediate consequence of destroying indigenous African economies, paving the way for a generalized syndrome of dependency. Nabudere claims that Africa's mining and metalworking capabilities and technology were superior to those of Europe and China. However, the only major evidence and documentation to support this assertion is provided by Greg Lanning and Marti Mueller (1979), who claim that African communities generally resisted the acquisition of their mineral resources by foreign interests, who consequently resorted to force and duplicity to gain their way. They also locate the beginnings of the unfair balance of economic relations between Africa and Europe in this situation. Also noteworthy is that the political and cultural equation required for harmonious existence prior to the imperialist intrusion has not been fully restored. Nabudere points out that this is particularly evident in the Great Lakes Region to the shame not only of the African continent but also of peoples of African descent in the diaspora.

While Nabudere is highly critical of the role played by European powers in the emasculation of Africa, he is no less disapproving of the part undertaken by Africans themselves within the contemporary moment in further undermining the beleaguered continent. During the earlier European scramble and Balkanization of the continent, Europeans played a decisive role in undermining the continent. However, after the attainment of political independence, Africans, in alliance with foreign interests and actors, have also been at the forefront of dismantling the political as well as territorial integrity of the continent. Nabudere finds this particular angle quite worrisome and his condemnation is unambiguous.

There is a slight difference between the colonial dismemberment of the Great Lakes Region and the contemporary onslaught it is experiencing in the sense that under the reign of King Leopold II of Belgium, the notion of oeuvre civilisatrice (civilizing work) was employed as the justification for the subjugation and "domestication" of Central Africa (Mudimbe 1988). However, as noted earlier, the real reason for the colonial subjugation of Africa in general and the Great Lakes in particular was for the purpose of economic exploitation. When it was no longer possible to dominate African colonies incorporating Burundi, Rwanda, and what is now known as the Democratic Republic of Congo (DRC), the colonial powers, in this case, Belgium, "scrambled out" just as quickly as they had ventured in, leaving the colonies in utter disarray and degradation.

This made it considerably difficult to administer and develop the newly freed territories. The situation left the territories vulnerable to civil war. In spite of it all, Belgium under Leopold II was not really interested in relinquishing its hold over what later became The Democratic Republic of Congo (DRC); it was only through a combination of its own mounting enfeeblement and the vigorous opposition to colonial rule that forced it out of the equation. But the vacuum left in the wake of Belgium's withdrawal was soon filled by American and French interests. Needless to add, these interests were usually inimical to those of indigenous inhabitants of the region. If the idea of *oeuvre civilisatrice* had been central to the colonial Balkanization of the Great Lakes Region, Nabudere states that the term under which contemporary foreign interests justify their invasion of the region is "globalization." Unfortunately, Nabudere does not elaborate upon this classification, which, under its current usage, is encumbered by numerous connotations both positive and negative.

Nonetheless, under the guise of globalization, foreign interests ostensibly attempt to bring about development within the region. Again, colonialist prejudice and implications of this self-serving sentiment are not difficult to discern. The racist portrayal of the Congo in Joseph Conrad's *Heart of Darkness* is evoked by Nabudere as a reminder of the tropes of denigration that are constantly applied to Africa as a site of squalor, madness, disease, decay, and death. Conrad's analogy is not exactly new and belongs within an established tradition of colonialist demonology in relation to Africa and its subjects. The analogy of black ants and Africans is not particularly new; it had already been in existence since Graeco-Roman imagery. Flavius Philostratus's *Icones* recounts the ordeal of Hercules on arrival in the ancient territory of Libya, where he was assailed by Pygmies, who descended upon him like a brigade of black ants.

These racist tropes have not entirely disappeared in contemporary times as demonstrated by an article Adam Hoschchild, entitled, "Mr. Kurtz, I Presume" (1997) which claims that the fictive Captain Kurtz in Conrad's famous novel is modeled after a true life character and actual circumstances that occurred in colonial times where Africans appeared as numerous and baleful as black ants. Hoschchild claims that Kurtz is a fictive manifestation of a Belgian military officer named Leon Rom. Again, at the height of the intense fighting that eventually forced the dictator Mobutu Sese Seko from the reins of power, the image of Kurtz is evoked as a symbol of resistance within a context of primitive savagery and meaningless (post)colonial violence. Of course, the figure of Laurent Kabila as the nemesis of Mobutu is intimately tied to the sordid circumstances that lead to the denouement of a major chapter in the political history of the DRC. A triumphant Kabila, (president of the DRC from 1997 until his assassination in 2001), fighting under the banner of the Alliance of Democratic Forces for the Liberation of Congo-Zaire (ADFL), ousted Mobutu, and in the parade of victory, opponents' heads were grazed by bullets and their bodies were dumped in mass graves. The barbarity of these gratuitous acts of victory recalls the acts of Belgians in Conrad's fictive tale, who decorated their gardens with the skulls of vanquished black people. Here, Nabudere is merely underlining the predictable recurrence of the tropes of barbarism associated with Africa and its seemingly unending cycle of conflicts.

As part of its cause for fighting, the ADFL had also claimed to be against the Interahamwe and Hutu rebels, who had been behind the Rwandan genocide of 1994. And yet they had perpetrated atrocities of similar magnitude with the support or at least the knowledge of European and American allies. The United States in particular endeavored to treat Kabila with kid gloves to install a major leader in the region with whom they could deal. American and European interests were largely keen to control the mineral resources in the DRC and Africa as a whole, which included, "84 per cent of the world's cobalt; 80 per cent of the gold and diamonds; 46 per cent of the vanadium; 37 per cent of the platinum; 33 per cent of the chromite; 32 per cent of the manganese; 29 per cent of the phosphate; 24 per cent of the antimony; 20 per cent of the copper; 21 per cent of the uranium and 10 per cent of the petroleum" (Nabudere 2004: 7).

For the purpose of exploiting the mineral resources of the DRC during the colonial era, the Belgian Societe Generale group of companies was in charge. On the eve of DRC independence, its monopoly of the economy was around seventy percent. Nabudere states that during the same period, "it controlled the production, export and processing of copper, cobalt, diamond, and uranium from the mines it owned and at the same time it had a virtual monopoly over water and rail transportation in the Congo Basin" (ibid., 8).

When the DRC gained independence in June 1960, the number of interests competing for control over its resources had increased significantly. For instance, Harry Oppenheiemer, of the Anglo-American Corporation (AAC), founded in 1917 by Sir Ernest Oppenheimer and the J. P. Morgan Company, had also become involved, all of which exponentially compounded the challenges of nation-building for the new country.

It was these same interests that conspired to have independent Prime Minister of the country, Patrice Lumumba, assassinated. Rather than allow Lumumba to embark on the arduous task of nation-building, foreign interests, who had their sights set on the enormous mineral wealth of the Congo, banded together to eliminate him as his independent comportment did not bode well for alien intervention and control.

The geopolitical situation was fraught as a result of an implacable East-West ideological confrontation that pitted the then Soviet Union and its allies against the United States and its collaborators. Lumumba was perceived by the West as favoring a socialist orientation and was, therefore, a threat to both its political as well as economic interests. Nabudere mentions that evidence exists to demonstrate the involvement of the American Central Intelligence Agency (CIA) in the murder of Lumumba. He states that there is a book in existence that claims the actual assassination of Lumumba was effected by a Belgian soldier who had acted on the instructions of superior officers. However, he fails to provide details of the book in question or provide evidence to support the veracity of its claims.

What Nabudere does instead is to point out that Lumumba's elimination began a spate of assassinations or assassination attempts involving African leaders who were either leftist in persuasion or who demonstrated an independent, and therefore uncontrollable, turn of mind. Specifically, he mentions leaders such as "Nasser of Egypt, Nkrumah of Ghana, Lumumba of Congo, Sukarno of Indonesia, Castro of Cuba, and Allende of Chile" (ibid., 10) as victims in various ways of drastic and undue Western interference.

Kwame Nkrumah had drawn attention to a document put together by the North Atlantic Treaty Organization (NATO) urging pro-West dissents in third world rebellions to endeavor to eliminate nationalist or pro-Soviet leaders in their regions (ibid., 11). It was accordingly necessary for Nkrumah to speak to Africans who belonged in the same ideological camp:

> We cannot afford either to ignore the sinister chain of interests which unites events in the Congo and Angola to East and South Africa. These interests are also connected with the East-West battle for world supremacy and the frenzied efforts being made to drag newly emerging countries of Africa into the orbit of the Cold War. The contest for ideological influence over the new states of Africa is throwing into confusion and complicating even more what is already a complex enough struggle from imperialist political and economic dominance and the unification of the continent. Any difference, any kind of fissure among Africans is seized and turned to the imperialist and Cold War interests (ibid.).

Nkrumah also decried the activities of *agent provocateurs*, such as Moise Tshombe, who were being employed as pawns to foster ethnic discontent by foreign powers motivated by Cold War ideological biases. It is in this light that the emergence of Mobutu should be construed. Lumumba had requested Soviet-supplied air transport to assist in sorting out the problems in Katanga, which revolved around the quest for the wresting of economic control of the Congo by foreign interests. The Kennedy administration, then in office in the United States, clashed with the Soviet Union over those interests. The United States needed a strong person as ruler of the mineral rich country and it appeared that neither Tshombe nor President Joseph Kasabuvu could provide the degree of dominance and control that was required, so the CIA threw its weight behind Mobutu, who assumed power on 24 November 1965.

Mobutu had first assumed the reins of power in the DRC as Army Chief of Staff, in 1960, after the assassination of Patrice Lumumba, which he subsequently relinquished. After a second coup in 1965, he assumed the presidency, and was determined to hold on to power with the backing of the United States. All he had to do in return was to provide an atmosphere of legality and order in the country. Mobutu renamed the DRC "Republic of Zaire" in 1971 (until 1997), and commenced his program of Zairian "national authenticity," during which he bought off the petty bourgeoisie to create a basis of uniting the Zairian people to serve as a bulwark for himself, personally.

Mobutu proceeded to nationalize Belgian economic interests in a way that did not threaten US interests. The policy of authenticity was selective in the manner in which it created an elite sect of economic compradors, often in alliance with their Belgian partners. Government focus was mainly directed at the urban centers, while the rural areas and agriculture were neglected. With agricultural production failing, Zaire resorted to importing food items from Southern Rhodesia (now called Zimbabwe) and thirty percent of its earnings from its mineral wealth was expended on food largely meant for its new class of urban economic denizens. Mobutu also oversaw the privatization of political authority, which enabled him to exert control over the much of Zaire's mineral wealth. In this way, he was able to amass a personal fortune of almost $10 billion USD toward the end of his reign. His main foreign backers, who acted within the context of the Cold War ideological conflict, notably the United States, France, and Belgium, turned a blind eye while he brazenly plundered his country.

Nabudere points out that the geopolitical realities of the Cold War created conditions for the emergence of rulers of Mobutu's ilk, who often served as pawns in the contestations between global superpowers. At the end of the Cold War, such rulers were no longer required as processes of contemporary globalization entailed a different ethos of governance. Mobutu had implemented an extensive policy of nationalization during the Cold War Era, which, under the succeeding global ideological and economic climate, was deemed obsolete. Instead of nationalization, economic liberalization and privatization was advocated by combined interests involving the Bretton Woods system of monetary management.

Under Belgian colonial administration, Zaire had accrued a national debt of $5 billion USD, which increased to $8 billion USD during the reign of Mobutu. The International Monetary Fund (IMF) and the World Bank pressured the Mobutu regime to undertake the privatization of state enterprises as an essential condition for more loans and debt servicing. Zaire was urged to undertake other drastic measures such as democratization, the withdrawal of subsidies and benefits from miners, and extensive cut-backs in public spending and social services. In short, what was being advocated was the effective dismemberment of the Zairian state.

International mining conglomerates were particularly in favor of the complete dissolution of the ineffectual Zairian state, which had become cumbersome and ineffective in advancing their interests. While the main actors of the Berlin

Conference at the beginning of the colonial era had instituted a different notion and structure of statehood, the global powers of the epoch of contemporary globalization advanced an ethic based on downsizing, which translated into monumental job losses creating grim sociopolitical and economic conditions in the process. As such, many African communities often resisted the trend to privatize and liberalize their economies.

In the meantime, international pressures mounted by the United States, Great Britain, and France to ensure the liberalization of the Zairian economy continued as new mining conglomerates entered the scene. Internal dissension against Mobutu's rule was also mounting. Rwanda, Zaire's neighbor, was also experiencing its own political crises that would eventually spill into Zaire and have severe and prolonged consequences. Uganda, also nearby, would become enmeshed in the political contestations occurring in both Zaire and Rwanda. Inherent in these various political contestations was a flagrant quest for profit by all parties concerned. Dissidents against the Mobutu regime needed the financial muscle gained through the mineral resources of the country to advance their sectional political agendas. Zaire's neighbors, taking advantage of its numerous internal problems and weaknesses, also had their eyes on the enormous mineral wealth of the country.

The weaknesses and inefficiency of Zaire were particularly acute. Provinces had become largely independent of the central state. The province of Shaba (Katanga) had even introduced its own currency. Even Kinshasa became an autonomous geographical and political entity as the central state crumbled inch-by-inch.

Even as he oversaw the dissolution of the Zairian state, Mobutu had also become arrogant toward the new global financial power brokers that operated out of Washington D.C., Paris, and Brussels. For instance, he resisted the privatization of the economy and instead, with the assistance of a few cronies, maintained it as his personal fiefdom. This approach was antithetical to those favored by the Bretton Woods system of monetary management and the new mineral prospecting conglomerates.

Thus, Mobutu attempted to assert his independence from the powerful Western interests keen to gain a control over his country's mineral riches, forgetting that he had once been their instrument in getting rid of Lumumba. In Nabudere's view, Mobutu's perceived historical value as an advocate of Western imperialism on the one hand, and as an ally of the West during the Cold War on the other, led to an often confusing ambivalence on the part of US authorities in dealing with him. Nabudere goes on to aver that there was, in fact, a certain degree of method behind the ambivalence.

The official US position was to turn a blind eye to the destructive activities of Rwandan and Ugandan forces on Zairian soil, while urging Mobutu to enter into dialogue with the armed rebels and dissidents, who were undermining Zaire's territorial integrity in a bid to establish an increasingly elusive peace. Nabudere captures the schizophrenic nature of such policy succinctly in saying, "while the CIA and US security agencies worked on the Uganda and Rwanda side to monitor the war and violence on their side at night, they talked the need for peace and dialogue during the day" (ibid., 17).

The United States had initially advised Mobutu to embark on an elaborate democratization process to end the political crises plaguing Zaire. But this position changed to requesting that he initiate negotiations with the increasingly assertive rebels intent on taking over the country. Eventually, according to Nabudere, the US position was further modified to calls for Mobutu to relinquish political power. For its part, Great Britain would not have minded the dismantling of the bloated Zairian state into smaller, more manageable geographical entities. As Mobutu's internal and international isolation grew, the United States on its own part, had been seriously contemplating the modus operandi by which a post-Mobutu arrangement would operate. Nabudere claims that the United States was well aware of Paul Kagame's massacre of Hutu indigenes in eastern Zaire. He also claims that the United States was intent on creating "princedoms" in Uganda, Rwanda, Ethiopia, and Zaire to take the place of the unwanted state-run mineral enterprises that existed under Mobutu's rule. Clearly, Mobutu had become yesterday's man and his unwillingness to adapt had been causing a great deal of frustration in international circles.

As noted, this frustration stemmed from the inability of foreign mining conglomerates to access without undue hindrance the mineral deposits of the Congo. Diamonds are found largely in the south eastern region of the country and in the eastern and western Kasai areas. These regions are responsible for about 70–80 percent of industrial minerals. An estimated 23.3 million carats with a combined value of 715 million US dollars were mined. Fresh diamond deposits had been discovered in the Kisangani region, which had attracted both Rwanda and Uganda. Zaire did not have the capacity to exploit these new mining opportunities and neither did its mining corporations, which were saddled with obsolete and inefficient equipment. Thus, both the politico-institutional and economic conditions in Zaire were not conducive to the internal exploitation of its immense mineral wealth.

At this juncture, Nabudere demonstrates his unambiguous anti-imperialist stance. Here, he argues that globalization is just another guise for colonial exploitation. After the termination of the Cold War era, the global ideological climate was reconfigured to accommodate the imperatives of globalization, under which gargantuan state structures and enterprises were deemed obsolete and market fundamentalism (sometimes termed the Washington Consensus) was encouraged. Such strategies were enforced in most parts of Africa and the Third World.

Apart from this alliance of major institutional partners, powerful individuals acting in private capacities also had enormous stakes in the global ideological-economic configuration. Nabudere writes:

> The new monopolies were a "new breed" of globalised business groups, some of them headed by monarchs, former politicians, military leaders, the new "make money quick and quit" investors as well as criminal elements seeking new opportunities where these could be had on the cheap. They all operated under the secretive umbrella organisation called the "Club of the Isles" which comprises the House of Windsor led by oligarchic institutions centred around a tightly knit alliance of European princely families, London-based financial and insurance houses, and food and raw materials cartels (ibid., 19).

Nabudere further highlights the reach and character of the emergent configuration of this global cartel of business interests by citing the *Executive Investigative Review* (EIR): "the "Club of Isles" worked closely and deployed the services of a global environmental movement called the World Wide Fund for Nature (WWF) headed by Philip, Duke of Edinburgh, the husband of Queen Elizabeth II, of England, and its funding arm called the "Club 101," which is also a propaganda and paramilitary arm of their One World "New Age Agenda (ibid.). Nabudere also mentions that "former President George H. W. Bush and former Canadian Prime Minister [Brian] Mulroney were reported by *Africa Confidential* to control these new conglomerates in Zaire" (ibid.). Nabudere goes on to equate Bush's imperial agenda with the earlier agenda of the main conveners of the Berlin Conference of 1884, also known as the Congo Conference, which regulated European colonization and trade in Africa during the New Imperialism period and formalized the "Scramble for Africa," and which overrode most existing forms of African autonomy and self-governance. This time around, however, the main beneficiaries of the plunder were interests brought together by global financial capital. Some of these global mining conglomerates include, an American/Canadian firm called Barrick Gold Corporation, a Toronto-based company called Banro Resources, a Belgian company known as Mines D'Or du Zaire (MDDZ), the Cluff Mining Company of London and the AAC. Some these business concerns, in particular, AAC, acquired military weapons to protect and secure their interests. Another corporation, American Mineral Fields (AMF), based in Arkansas and operated from Canada, intended to deal in minerals of the very best quality. A major shareholder of AMF, Jean-Raymonde Boulle, who owned another company, American Diamond Buyers, forked out 25,000 US dollars to Laurent Kabila's militia to gain a trading license in minerals when it had not fully secured power. In a similar vein, Consolidated Eurocan, a Vancover based company bought "a 55 percent stake in Gécamines's Tenke-Fungurume copper-cobalt deposits, which were located in Shaba province" (ibid., 22), which accounted for the largest amount of its kind in the world.

Western corporations were not the only ones angling to exploit and despoil the mineral resources of the region. Iskor Ltd. (now Mittal Steel) and Gencor Ltd., which were South African mining corporations, allied with a British raw material syndicate were also involved.

Nabudere is of the view that the collective efforts of these predatory corporations suggest that there was an overall design to dismember Zaire and have multinational corporations run its broken down geographical units. The EIR specifically mentions that AAC sought to dismantle Zaire and have it reduced to a mere colony to be administered under postmodern conditions. AAC, considered the largest mineral dealing concern in the world, together with the Barrick Gold Corporation, the largest gold mining concern in the world, operated its concessions in the Great Lakes Region with Ugandan, Rwandan, and Zimbabwean forces. The human costs of the activities of these various mining corporations were enormous as they destroyed traditional means of livelihood, created hunger and famine, and displaced huge numbers of people without providing any safety nets.

Many companies were dealing with Kabila even before there had been any definite political outcome with regard to his rebellion. This, in turn, meant that these various business concerns were prepared to conduct business with whomever was in power in any given region at any given time, and not necessarily Kabila himself. In other words, they were willing to undermine the sovereignty and territorial integrity of any African nation as long as it suited their immediate financial interests. The corporations were in effect, poised to act in lieu of traditional structures of governance, only in this case, they were not accountable to the populations that fell under their control. Here, Nabudere advances perhaps his most significant conceptual insight when he writes:

> This is what the recolonization process called globalization came to mean for Zaire. The idea was to "deconstruct" the old European colonial states if necessary and create new ethnically based mini-states. This represented a new policy of divide and rule under new conditions. The British and other economic monopolies seemed to be eagerly pushing this scenario. But this recolonisation was taking new shape by disintegrating the old post-colonial states and replacing them with new principalities headed by new breed princes. (ibid., 23)

The Washington Consensus supported this scenario, which also required the involvement of a select group of African leaders, of which Yoweri Museveni of Uganda was a key figure. Museveni was an autocrat who pursued the neoliberal ideals of market fundamentalism. He had also led his country through what had been previously considered an unimaginable growth path, achieving in the process an 8.5 percent annual growth rate. Coupled with this impressive rate of growth was an intensive program of privatization, in which foreign interests gained whatever control they wished over the economy. This made Museveni and

Kagame of Rwanda important allies for Western economic interests. Regarding Museveni, Nabudere writes:

> Clearly, the US saw in Museveni someone who would play the role of a regional power broker on behalf of the Anglo-American alliance. The US was in favour of the emergence of a "new breed" of African leaders that supported the US sponsored "Washington Consensus" as part of its globalization strategy. Museveni had already embraced these reforms, which made it easier for the alliance to redraw the map of Africa in the post-Cold War period. Museveni did not want Kagame to emerge as a challenger to that role (ibid., 25).

Supporters of the Washington Consensus sought to impose its principles in Africa, and in so doing, enlist the participation of African leaders such as Museveni. The Consensus policies upheld the ethics of good governance, fiscal responsibility, trade liberalization, competitive exchange rates, infrastructure investment, and privatization of state enterprises. Of course, it did not occur to the foreign diplomats who endeavored to employ these policies that their supposed virtues ran counter to the aspirations of African peoples who merely wished to be free of intrusive and manipulative foreign interference in their daily affairs.

Museveni is indeed a contradictory figure. He has been called "a patron of Zairian rebels" and a man who is "more conservative than Margaret Thatcher" (ibid.). He is also exceedingly ambitious in seeking to forge an alliance of like-minded African leaders who would pursue a foreign-guided program of development for the region. The irony of Museveni's position and activities is not new. It recalls the trajectory of Mobutu as a Western pawn. Not surprisingly, Museveni also harbors a personal agenda that may not necessarily be Western-supported. He seeks to re-establish the Chwezi dynasty that would be largely shaped by Hima and Tutsi regional dominance. Another curiosity in Museveni's position is that he is one of Africa's longest serving rulers, which undercuts America's stated belief in democracy. Autocracy and not democracy is Museveni's preferred political creed.

Mobutu had operated on the basis of state-owned and managed enterprises and this situation created a particular agglomeration of interests as well as alliances. As the ideological scenario altered, a new aggregation of interests and alliances took shape and challenged the old order, sapping the Mobutu regime of its vitality and relevance. Under the ideology of neoliberalism, it has been pointed out that ambitious rebel lords cannot afford to act alone, as this is likely to end in violent ethnic conflict. Museveni, Kagame and their collaborators were of the view that the only way to achieve meaningful political dominance and stability would be by seeking fruitful alliances with well-resourced foreign interests. This prognosis obviously has dire implications for the notion of African sovereignty and ultimately, agency.

Indeed, the reality is perhaps even more disconcerting. Foreign companies venture into African territories, buying up mineral rich regions, which they then exploit for their own benefit. African workers are employed with slave wages and the rest of the population is promptly ignored without social services and infrastructure. In other words, they are left to the elements, and random violence and outbreaks of war are instigated.

The British imperial view attempted to present yet another argument in relation to Zaire. Zaire was deemed too large to manage and it was better to allow it to disintegrate while its warring peoples attempted to reach some degree of understanding of what shape it would eventually assume after its geographical and administrative collapse.

Some foreign analysts had argued that a quicker way to avoid the prolongation of the Zairian conflict was to discourage its internationalization. But the real situation presented a contrary scenario. As violence within Zaire intensified, refugees from the country spilled into neighboring countries such as Uganda. Even before the Zairian crisis mushroomed at the tail end of the Mobutu era, the entire geographical region was bedeviled with a myriad of lingering unresolved conflicts, which lay in varying states of dormancy.

For instance, in November 1978, Idi Amin, the Ugandan ruler, had invaded the Kagera Valley in Tanzania thereby provoking counter military action. Idi Amin had mounting internal opposition to his dictatorial rule back at home and so it was not unexpected that the Ugandan National Liberation Front (UNLF) joined forces with the Tanzanian Peoples Defence Forces (TPDF) in warding off Amin's military onslaught. The combined forces were not only able to rebuff him but also eventually had him deposed. Yusufu Lule took Amin's place as head of state. Meanwhile, Yoweri Museveni, who had been involved with the drive to topple Amin was rapidly consolidating his military position even as he worked under Lule as minister of state for defense and after the civilian administration was deposed as Vice-Chairman of the Uganda Military Commission. He had acquired the support of segments within the TPDF as well as Banyankole indigenes and Tutsi refugees which he would put to use in his subsequent military campaigns.

In December 1980, elections were held under the watch of the Uganda Military Commission. Milton Obote's the Uganda People's Congress emerged victorious in what was generally perceived as a botched election. Museveni then embarked on guerrilla warfare as a way of settling his grievance with the Obote administration. Many of Museveni's troops were drawn from sections within the National Army for the Liberation of Uganda (NALU) comprising Ankole and Rwandan ethnic indigenes. Once the guerrilla campaign had been launched Museveni's forces became known as the Popular Revolutionary Army (PRA) and then subsquently as the National Resistance Movement and Army (NRM/A). This army gained control of the "Luwero Triangle" in Uganda which was populated by Tutsi refugees from Rwanda and other immigrants from which the NRM/A derived its members who came in handy in opposing the Obote administration.

The Rwandan indigenes within the NRM/A subsequently compelled Museveni to support their invasion of their home country, Rwanda, which was then governed by President Juvénal Habyarimana. This was possible because Rwandan military commanders held signficant positions in the Museveni regime between 1986–1989 and were able to amass the necessary machinery and weaponry to implement their plan. It is well known that Kagame, leading the Rwandan Patriotic Army (RPA) secured military equipment and amoured tanks with the promise to return them to Uganda once through with them. Museveni started to entertain expansionist intentions regarding a large portion of the Great Lakes Region in which he came to perceive Rwanda, Burundi, and eastern Zaire as constituting part of East Africa. Rwanda, under Kagame, voiced its support for another colonialist Berlin conference to settle the perennial problem of Africa's conflictual territoriality. In the Ugandan/Rwanda case, the major source of conflict can be traced to Belgian military occupation of the Great Lakes Region during World War I. A *coup d'état* hatched by Hutu plotters, in 1959, drove an influx of Tutsi immigrants into Uganda some of whom were later utilized by Museveni in orchestrating his military campaigns.

Uganda often invaded and held on to territories in Zaire under the pretext that it was attempting to flush out rebels acting within the Allied Democratic Forces (ADF), a Muslim fundamentalist force wreaking havoc in the Kasese and Bundibugyo districts of Uganda. Ugandan invasions of eastern Zaire worked well with new US mining interests operating in the country.

At this juncture, Nabudere requests a deeper interpretation of Ugandan involvement in the Zairian crisis. His argument is that there was a fortuitous but mutually beneficial convergence of interests between the regimes of Rwanda and Uganda on the one hand, and the different emergent global economic agglomerations intent on the exploitation of the area, on the other. Nabudere, has unsparing words for his fellow compatriot, Museveni, whose activities in the region have done much to destabilize the peace:

> Museveni... saw matters from a narrow perspective and the maintenance of personal political power, the taking over of these territories would ensure the expansion of his political power into that of a regional power-broker. To him the suffering of the people of these regions was of little concern as long as he achieved his ambitions, forgetting that Mobutu had also been used to engage in those kinds of dreams and ambitions (ibid., 30).

A foreign minister (whom Nabudere fails to name) of the DRC (Kabila reverted the name after taking power in 1997) complained at a meeting of the Security Council of United Nations (UN) that both Uganda and Rwanda were engaged in a mass scale and illegal plunder of the mineral resources of his country. Such complaints about looting continued to emerge from various quarters within the DRC. Both Uganda and Rwanda had initially professed to be liberators of the

DRC from its myriad political ills, but had gone onto enforce a different sort of captivity upon it. Some of the looting extracted from the DRC included, "unprocessed coffee, timber, minerals such as gold and diamonds and saps (sic) from rubber as well as petroleum products" (ibid., 32). The people of the DRC continually decried the sorry state to which their country had fallen, saying "the price is being paid by the Congolese people who are not only being killed the process" (33), and, as such, they moaned:

> what kind of "liberators" are these who claim they are there to train Congolese to fight Kabila in order to bring democracy to their country, when they themselves have no transparent systems of governance in their countries. (ibid.)

The problems of the DRC are not the only ones that hamper stability in the Great Lakes Region. Rwanda has its own chronic internal tensions that continue to threaten the overall tranquility of the region. The 1994 Rwandan genocide had been, in part, provoked by the shooting down of the plane in which Rwandan President Habyarimana had been traveling killing him and his Burundian counterpart, President Cyprien Ntaryamira. As a result, Hutu indigenes embarked on a murderous path of vengeance killing more than 800,000 individuals during the brief period of the massacre. Nabudere mentions that Habyarimana had been killed on the orders of the leader of the Rwandan Patriotic Front (RPF), Kagame. Kagame then launched a drive to seize power in Rwanda, which in turn led to large numbers of Hutu indigenes (some estimates state more than two million people) seeking refuge in eastern Zaire to avoid Tutsi retaliatory ire. Among this deluge of Hutu immigrants were members of the murderous Interahamwe rebel group, a Hutu paramilitary organization, who had been largely behind the Rwandan genocide.

Mahmood Mamdani (2001) had argued that Belgian colonial misrule has a lot to answer for in relation to the 1994 Rwandan catastrophe. Previously, Hutu and Tutsi indigenes had lived quite peacefully together until the artificial Belgian idea of ethnic classification and division had created misplaced antimony in both ethnicities. This mutual distrust and hatred continued into the postcolonial period and eventually culminated in the genocide, after which they were driven out of Rwanda, mostly into Zaire. When Kagame was installed to power, Rwandan troops started to infiltrate Zaire to destroy remnants of the Interahamwe militia, some of whom were to be found in refugee camps harboring Hutu immigrants. The Interahamwe continued to entertain plans of invading Rwanda and deposing Kagame in return.

Kagame employed the fact that the militia was still active in Zaire as reason to collaborate with foreign interests, who had decided that Mobutu was more of liability than an asset. As such, Kagame was in pursuit of the Interahamwe in Zaire as Mobutu rapidly lost his allies within Africa and beyond. But as we have noted, apart from the immediate military threat posed by rebels based in

Zaire, Rwanda, just as Uganda, was keenly interested in gaining free access of the mineral deposits in the country.

The United States soon came out to support both Uganda and Rwanda, whose troops often ventured into Zaire, thereby violating its sovereignty. The US Secretary of State, Madeline Albright, called Museveni, "a beacon of hope" in Africa while she declared, "Rwanda is to the US what the pupil is to the eye" (Nabudere 2004: 36). The Rwandan army even received military training from US forces, and Uganda was bolstered in its fight against the Islamic regime in the Republic of the Sudan. Kabila, on his part, benefited from Ugandan and Rwandan support in his drive to flush out Mobutu from power. Accounts were later produced attesting to direct American military involvement along with Ugandan, Rwandan, and Kabila's militia in the deposition of Mobutu. At its onset, Kabila's armed onslaught was known as the Banyamulenge rebellion. Accordingly:

> the US established training facilities at a place called Kabamba in western Uganda where US instructors trained both Ugandan and Kabila forces, just before the "rebellion" broke out. Later in 1997, [3rd] Special Forces [Group (Airborne)] from Fort Bragg in the United States was sent to supplement the training. After this training some 700 Ugandan troops were issued with American-made uniforms, night vision goggles, and sophisticated equipment (ibid., 37).

Kabila's opposition to the Mobutu regime dates as far back as the 1960s, when he founded the Parti de la Revolution Populaire (PRP), which encountered many setbacks in defeating Mobutu. Kabila reckoned that he needed to provide an appropriate ideological basis on which his movement would operate. This ideological orientation drew upon the precepts of Maoism/Marxism/Leninism, and Kabila at one point was able to depend on the support of famed revolutionary, Che Guevara. However, the movement, which had developed modes of self-sufficiency, was largely confined to the mountains of Uvira-Fizi as it lacked the wherewithal to venture forth.

Nabudere then poses a vital question: How was it possible for Kabila, previously cut off in the mountains, to transform himself into Mobutu's nemesis and by so doing, become at a critical moment – and only for that moment – a figure of liberation in his problematic country? In order to better understand the ramifications of this question and adduce possible responses to it, the Banyamulenge rebellion needs to be addressed.

Indeed, the rebellion may explain much of what Nabudere terms Africa's first world war. The origins of the Banyamulenge rebellion can be traced to the era of colonial occupation spanning several countries in the Great Lakes Region. Primarily, these countries include Rwanda, Burundi, Uganda, Angola, Republic of the Sudan, and of course, the Congo within the African continent. Beyond the continent, France, Belgium, Great Britain, and the United States are all involved with varying degrees of culpability for fueling the Banyamulenge rebellion. The Banyamulenge ethnic phenomenon emerged as the result of Belgian colonial high-handedness, in which Tutsis of Rwandan origin were caught up in the Congo. They were later joined by refugees from Rwanda and Burundi, who were fleeing from violence in their respective areas, all of whom were said to have settled "between the Lake Kivu and Tanganyika or between Bukavu and Unvira in the south Kivu province of Zaire" (ibid., 40). Rwandan Hutu and Tutsi indigenes were also to be found in south-western Uganda during the colonial period. Between 1937 and 1955, Belgian colonial authorities relocated "thousands of Banyarwanda peasants to the eastern districts of Masisi, Rutshuru and Walikalema" in Kivu in order to alleviate the density of the population in Rwanda.

After Mobutu assumed power, some of the Rwandan and Burundian immigrants in Zaire had secured significant positions within the Zairian sociopolitical and economic hierarchy and were able to push for citizenship in 1972. This caused a lot of antimony within the local population and was eventually effectively resisted in 1981, when the decree extending citizenship to Rwandan and Burundian immigrants was reversed. Consequently, the former citizens were reduced to stateless people. They were also stripped of lands that the local population regarded as ancestral property. And so, to a large extent, Mobutu can be said to have supplied the fuel for the Banyamulenge rebellion. But there are other noteworthy angles to the phenomenon as well. For instance, Uganda admitted refugees of Rwandan origin in 1959, 1963, and 1973. In 1972, more than 70,000 Hutus from Burundi fled widespread violence for Tanzania where they were granted citizenship. These forced migrations into these various countries would in time have a number of implications for regional peace and stability and in some cases, their consequences were dire.

The Banyamulenge ethnic community in Zaire was decisive in the drive to rid Mobutu of political power. Kabila had employed the ethnic community in his struggles with Mobutu and he was eventually able to succeed. But on gaining power, he turned his back on the Banyamulenge and appeared to encourage xenophobic sentiments in his country. Once again, the Banyamulenge found themselves in the same situation in which they had been during the nefarious Mobutu regime, when they were rendered stateless. Their statelessness correlates with the vacuous entity the Zairian state became after several decades of abuse, neglect, and constant tumult. But the widespread violence was not limited to Zaire alone. The RPF government in Rwanda, in its bid to annihilate the Hutu Interahamwe rebels internally as well as those based in eastern Zaire, is deemed to have conducted a policy of genocide not only against the rebels but also against moderate Tutsis opposed to the regime. Uganda, for its part, experienced a series of revolts in the western region, which the government, in attempting to quell, displaced 25,000 Ugandans, who were forced to seek refuge in eastern Zaire, where they joined the Interahamwe rebels in opposing the Museveni government. So, in Zaire, Uganda, Rwanda, and Burundi there were chronic dissent and unrest that could flare out of proportion at any given time.

In Zaire, the Banyamulenge continued to press for citizenship while Kabila bowed to wishes of the Zairian population stating that the matter had to be decided in a constitutional assembly, which, of course, caused dismay and resentment among the immigrants. Rwanda accused him of encouraging the Interahamwe located in Zaire. Rwanda also accused him of not honoring the agreement made with him before the overthrow of Mobutu where he pledged to cede parts of Zaire to Rwanda. Rather than explore the ways in which the disagreement could be resolved, he took to relying on his own ethnic group, the Baluba of Katanga, for personal security.

The Banyamulenge rebellion flared up again when they were not granted their request of citizenship after all their efforts to get rid of Mobutu, thereby paving the way for the emergence of Kabila. When they were not granted their request, they resolved not to take military instructions from non-Banyamulenge indigenes, which, in turn, created a situation of two running armies within the country. This had the potential of dividing up the country.

Kabila then tried to break up the partnership he had with Ugandan and Rwandan armed forces, stating that he was grateful for the assistance for which they had been paid in hard currency; then invited them to leave his country. Both Uganda and Rwanda were not pleased by his kind of gratitude and gathered in the northern and eastern parts of the DRC. The stage was clearly set for a confrontation, which began in 1998.

Uganda had more important motives for seeking a confrontation with Kabila's forces. In the preceding period of conflict in pre-Kabila Zaire, Uganda had secured possession of some mines in the country and was not about to give them up. Great Britain and the United States provided tacit support for Uganda and Rwanda, stating that they had the right to protect their security interests. With this in mind, the two countries set about getting rid of Kabila just as they had been instrumental in deposing Mobutu. Kabila requested for a conference to settle the matter, but both countries turned him down. Nabudere reports that the airlifting of Ugandan and Rwandan armed personnel was conducted by NATO. However, in spite of the assistance, the joint Ugandan and Rwandan military operation proved abortive due to the involvement of Zimbabwean, Angolan, and Namibian armed forces.

The Ugandans and Rwandans who wanted to depose Kabila believed that they needed a bona fide motive for their intention as opposed to just settling upon the Banyamulenge rebellion as a reason for intervention. For that purpose, a rebel movement was formed, named the Resemblement Congolais pour la democratic (RCD), made up of twenty-eight groups and two leaders, Ernest

Wamba dia Wamba and Arthur Z'ahidi Ngoma, whom Nabudere claims had the backing of the United States, Belgium, and France. The rebel movement was ultimately not popular among the Congolese, who viewed it as an organization closely allied to foreign interests. Those within the movement were, therefore, called collaborators or "collabos" in local parlance. Eventually, internal friction splintered the movement with some of its members going off with Wamba dia Wamba to become known as the RCD-Kisangani (RCD-K) faction. Another much bigger faction, the RCD-Goma, with connections with the Banyamulenge leadership and ties with Rwanda, had Émile Ilunga as its leader. Both factions of the RCD were largely controlled by Uganda and Rwanda, who manipulated them to suit their strategic interests. Rwanda demonstrated its readiness to intervene decisively if and when its interests were threatened. It instigated the removal of Ilunga as leader of the RCD-Goma faction and installed Adolophe Onsumba after RCD-Goma suffered a defeat in the hands of Kabila's forces.

Uganda, for its part, first of all, sought to gain control of the northern parts of DRC and secure unfettered access to the Atlantic Ocean. In order to do so, Uganda manipulated ethnic divisions primarily through RCD-K, so that no faction would become too powerful. Nabudere claims that both Wamba dia Wamba and Ilunga allowed themselves to be manipulated by their respective foreign backers. Wamba dia Wamba comes up for mention a few times for having struck deals with foreign interests to manage and control the revenues deriving from mineral extraction in the Kisangani area. In this regard, Van A. Brink, a US national, who was the founder of the First International Bank of Grenada (FIBG), secured the authority to manage the funds of the Kisangani region through Wamba dia Wamba's cooperation.

The RCD-Goma faction was also entangled in deals involving elaborate companies, Anglo-American and well-placed individuals such as Lunda Bululu, who was once a prime minister in the Mobutu regime. Rwanda has mining interests located in northern parts of the DRC, which is traditionally viewed as Uganda's sphere of interest. This had led to violent clashes between the two countries. Ultimately, the interventions of Uganda and Rwanda have not exactly been motivated by altruistic reasons, but rather to gain access to the DRC's mineral wealth, which, in turn, has led to spiraling violence and underdevelopment. As a smokescreen, both countries claim they are in the DRC to protect their legitimate security concerns with the backing of the United States and Great Britain.

The greed of Uganda and Rwanda attracted the involvement of several other African countries in the DRC. Zimbabwe, South Africa, Angola, Namibia, Chad, and to some extent, Sudan have all been involved in varying degrees with the conflict in the DRC. Cameroon, Gabon, and Libya have also been linked, if only marginally, to the conflict. Thus, Nabudere's thesis that the conflict essentially forms Africa's first world war is derived from this seemingly intractable nexus of conflicts and foreign interventions. Accordingly, he argues:

For the DRC, the struggle was for survival as a single state entity. For its leaders, it was a terminal war not only of the state, but along with it all the opportunities for patronage, neo-patrimonialism and power. It appeared as if the post-colonial states in Africa were consuming themselves in new "proxy wars" for those who were interested in Africa's gold and diamonds. These old and new mineral conglomerates were calling the tune and paying the piper. The war became not only bloody for the people of the region but a truly "bloody diamonds war." (ibid., 52)

Nabudere focuses quite distinctly on Zimbabwe's involvement in the DRC crisis, which, in his view, has a strong element of imperialism, albeit from an unexpected angle. Unlike Rwanda and Uganda, Zimbabwe has not been an ally of Great Britain and the United States due to its radical land reforms that have entailed seizing land from rich white farm owners in order to redistribute to poor Zimbabwean peasants. Robert Mugabe, president of Zimbabwe since 1980, claims that his country's intervention in the DRC is based on the fact that the latter belongs to the Southern African Development Community (SADC) and so is entitled to the region's collective assistance when in distress.

Nabudere is piqued by the fact that the IMF and the World Bank scrutinizes Zimbabwe's financial books to see if too much money has been expended on the DRC conflict while exempting Uganda and Rwanda, who have been the primary countries involved in the conflict. In Nabudere's view, the attitudes of the IMF and the World Bank toward Zimbabwe suggest a clear case of double standards and imperialism. Nabudere also points out that Zimbabwe's intervention is geared toward protecting and maintaining the territorial integrity of the DRC, as opposed to Uganda and Rwanda, who, together with their foreign backers, would rather see it splintered. Consequently, Laurent Kabila offered Zimbabwe mining concessions as payment for its services. Zimbabwe was not able to effectively exploit these concessions because it lacked the prerequisite skills and resources.

In addition, in 1998, Angola decided the DRC was of vital importance to its strategic interests. Angola also has its own checkered history similar to the DRC. During the Cold War, the People's Movement for the Liberation of Angola (MPLA) government had sided with the Eastern Bloc, which made it an enemy of the Western countries and their allies. Internally, Angolan political and military leader Jonas Savimbi's National Union for the Total Independence of Angola (UNITA), the rebel movement opposed to the MPLA, benefited tremendously from Western countries, who wanted to see an end to MPLA's communist-supported dominance.

To fuel its war against the MPLA government after the end of the Cold War, UNITA resorted to illegal mining and trading. As such, it had South African business collaborators, even during the period of apartheid, whom it employed in securing arms and ammunition in exchange for precious stones. UNITA bypassed all manner of international sanctions prohibiting trade in precious stones and arms, thereby compounding the violence in a number of African theaters of conflict, most notably Angola and the DRC. Between 1994–1997, Savimbi's UNITA, through an agreement with Mobutu, secured large arsenals from Eastern Europe. UNITA increasingly resorted to more clandestine and desperate measures to amass arms necessary for pursuing its conflict with the MPLA government in Luanda after its Western backers had abandoned its cause at the end of the East/West ideological conflict. UNITA's involvement in the DRC crisis was particularly messy given the fact that it opposed the MPLA government and was forced to operate actively outside Angola. Mobutu, at first, was a supporter of UNITA, which had to rethink its alliances after the Zairian ruler was abandoned by his erstwhile Western allies. General Gnassingbé Eyadéma (president of Togo from 1967 until his death in 2005), was then bribed by Savimbi with a small horde of diamonds to allow UNITA to import arms and ammunition through Togo.

Namibia, in time, also became interested in DRC's mineral deposits, thereby complicating an already fraught situation. As such, in July 1999, the Lusaka Peace Accord was signed in an attempt to bring a lasting solution to the DRC crisis. The accord took into account two main concerns: the internal context of conflict within the DRC and the security concerns of external parties enmeshed in the crisis.

The entanglement of Rwanda and Uganda in the crisis required particularly expert handling given their protracted and multi-faceted activities in the DRC. Nabudere adds that in order to alleviate the situation, "a comprehensive disarmament, demobilisation, resettlement and reintegration programme" (ibid., 64) of the external troops, which amounted to significant numbers, would be necessary. However, Uganda refused to comply with the terms of the peace accord; instead, it supported the disruptive activities of rebel militias within the DRC.

Another problem that prevented the implementation of the peace accord was the unavailability of the required funds as the UN was unable to raise the necessary material resources. On the military front, Ugandan and Rwandan troops clashed, resulting in the killing of about 200 Ugandan troops in Kisangani. Savimbi's UNITA continued to be a problematic presence in the region; it supported the drive to oust Kabila in opposition to the MPLA administration, which shielded him.

Also militating against the implementation of the Lusaka Peace Accord was the drive by multiple external parties and forces to lay hands on DRC's mineral wealth – most of all, Uganda and Rwanda. Ingrained in this quest were auxiliary activities pertaining to the acquisition of arms and ammunition, which only served to compound an already unmanageable situation.

After the assassination of Kabila and the collapse of the Lusaka Peace Accord, the Inter-Congolese Dialogue was initiated to address a number crucial issues within the DRC, namely: the humanitarian, social, and economic needs of the country; a credible electoral process; a constitution laying the groundwork for the institution of democracy; and finally, a solution to the perennial problem of the demobilization and disarmament of the various armed groups involved in the conflict. However, the Inter-Congolese Dialogue initiative encountered a major stumbling-block when Rwanda objected, stating that the effort was only meant to entrench the political position of President Joseph Kabila (who took office in 2001 after the death of his father, Laurent) while ignoring the needs and demands of all other groups involved in the conflict. Rwanda's Paul Kagame, expressed his opposition to the means and methods of achieving lasting peace in the DRC, thereby impeding the gains of the initiative. Apart from Kagame's resistance to the peace process, as mentioned before, the involvement of numerous countries and factions including multinational – British, American, Canadian, and Belgian – mining concerns made the quest for peace in the DRC a particularly tortuous process.

The Ugandan and Rwandan contestation over the mineral wealth of the DRC on the one hand, and the approaches by which the conflict might be resolved, on the other, led to acrimonious confrontations between both countries. Yoweri Museveni, President of Uganda since 1986, claimed that Rwanda preferred direct interference in the internal problems of the DRC, while his country favored a much less involved approach to the crisis, thereby creating much antagonism between the two countries. Uganda was keen to assume the more or less unchallenged position as a regional power, which Rwanda resisted, maintaining that it had its own legitimate interests in the DRC independent of Ugandan meddling.

Nabudere places the Ugandan and Rwandan squabbling over the mineral wealth of the DRC against a much broader canvas, incorporating Western powers that demand unfettered access to Africa's natural wealth. So rather than the supposed wealth creating actual material advancement, growth, and development, it has instead become the bane of the African continent. In the quest to acquire the continent's natural resources, entire populations are plunged into chaos and violence causing enormous humanitarian crises.

Nabudere also dwells on the famed dimensions of "blood diamonds," which encompass several levels of complicity. There is a high global demand for diamonds that are found in large quantities in Africa. Diamonds possess certain rare qualities such as being the purest gems known; their ability to retain and reflect light and radiance is especially unique. They are also the hardest substance to be encountered and cannot be cut by another tough substance such as steel. Only a diamond can successfully cut another diamond. It is said that the best diamonds in the world are to be found in Africa's alluvial mines. Paradoxically, the countries and regions in which they are located have been the sites of brutal and chronic violence and considerable immiseration of the populations involved. Yerodia Abdoulaye Ndombasi, the foreign minister of the DRC during the height of the global outcry against the so-called "blood diamonds, complained that his country was rapidly been smothered by the rapacity of "gemocrats."

Blood diamonds or conflict diamonds are not always easy to define. A loose definition claims that conflict diamonds "originate from areas in Africa controlled by forces fighting the legitimate and internationally recognized government of the relevant country" (ibid.81). However, the transportation of conflict diamonds goes through stable and apparently conflict-free zones, thereby blurring the lines by which an accepted definition of the term may apply. Nabudere points out that the standard definition of conflict diamonds is problematic since there are layers of complexity encompassing various channels, countries, firms, and actors. Accordingly:

> these diamonds are traded by large companies that have been involved in the mining of stones such as De Beers; government bodies selling official production; companies licensed to buy diamonds mined by others; small-scale mining companies selling their own production; licensed buyers; unlicensed buyers buying unlicensed production; and extensive trading in diamonds bourses and between companies or individuals. These diverse actors make it impossible to trace the "soaking up" of blood diamonds from conflict situations. (ibid., 83)

The end of the Cold War created new conditions under which arms could be traded to fuel contexts of conflict. The combination of blood diamonds and arms has, in turn, spurred the spread of globalized criminal syndicates dealing in both commodities. Analysts have noted that these highly networked syndicates are capable of undermining the functioning and stability of many nation-states, thus posing a severe threat to global security.

Within Africa, and particularly in the DRC and Angola, the scramble for diamonds is the cause of what Nabudere continually terms Africa's first world war. In the era of King Leopold II of Belgium, the prime commodities for colonial plunder and human enslavement had been gold and rubber and the similarities between the two historical epochs are quite clear. Repeatedly, Nabudere mentions that diamonds in Africa are a curse rather than a blessing, a situation akin to the plight caused by oil in contemporary Africa leading to what is known as the "Dutch Disease." This syndrome alludes to the prevalence of mineral wealth generating widespread poverty and even sometimes, societal chaos and destruction. Unfortunately, Africans themselves are very much involved in the annihilation of their communities in conjunction with their foreign collaborators. As such, comparisons have been made between African and European modes and effects of colonialism. Some have claimed that European colonialism introduced vital cash crops such as cotton, coffee and cocoa into local economies, thereby prompting their rapid expansion. African instances of internal colonization pursued by countries such as Rwanda, Uganda, Angola, Namibia, and Zimbabwe, on the other hand, have only pillage to report as their contribution to the DRC.

Meanwhile, the DRC is effectively being rendered useless as there is a concerted effort to divest it of its sovereignty, legitimacy, and power so that the combination of interests seeking to gain control of the country's wealth can have its way. These various interests, which often bypass the terms and conditions of legality, employ a seemingly legal language and façade to perpetrate acts of plunder, pillage, and ruthless economic exploitation. Nabudere is unequivocal in his condemnation of the contemporary African plight:

> Africa being at the bottom of the world system and rich in mineral resources is a victim of these global forces and unless it is able to put its own house in order, it will continue to be preyed upon by these global mafia-like forces in which some African elites are part because they benefit from it. The people of Africa must not accept the consequences of these forces that are exploiting the weaknesses of the continent. They must reorganize themselves in stable political institutions that can lead to an African reawakening and recovery in which Africans can assert their control over their own resources (ibid., 103).

This excerpt reveals a great deal of Nabudere's thought on Africa. Although there is an evident streak of pan-Africanism, it is not couched in the usual romanticism and sentimentality that often attend pan-Africanist views. First, Nabudere agrees that Africa maintains the least enviable position within the global system. Second, he identifies the need to build the continent until it acquires the desired strength. Third, he condemns the continent's elite classes, which have exploited and benefited from its deficiencies. This stance distances Nabudere from the sentimentalist school of pan-Africanism. Throughout the monograph, he is extremely critical of Uganda's role – as led by Yoweri Museveni – in the escalation of the DRC crises.

A decade after Nabudere's study, not much has changed in the DRC. The state is perennially weak and its territories remain subject to endemic violence and rampant warlordism. Various rebel groups, sometimes backed by Uganda and Rwanda and sometimes acting independently, continue to terrorize local populations raping women and children in the process. In the DRC, chaos and violence have remained entrenched. General Sikuli Lafontaine, the leader of *Union des Patriotes Congolais pour la Paix* (UPCP/FPC), a rebel militia, rules the areas around Bunyatenge, a village in the eastern part of the country. He had deserted the Congolese national army because he disapproved of Kabila's government taking along with him a sizeable number of troops. To fuel his rebellion, Lafontaine has thousands of men working in mines. Apart from being an enemy of Kabila, Lafontaine is also opposed to the *Forces démocratiques de libération du Rwanda* (FDLR), which has taken over from the M23 (which takes its name from the 23 March 2009 CNDP-DRC government peace treaty) as perhaps the major rebel militia impeding the quest for peace within the DRC.

The FDRL consists of Rwandan Hutus, who had been involved in the 1994 genocide. They remain stranded within the DRC, creating mayhem in the communities in which they reside. They are unable to return to Rwanda because of their past history, but the Kabila government has not demonstrated it possesses the required muscle to flush them out of the country. Even if the government succeeds in eventually halting its activities within the DRC, it is generally believed another rebel group would assume its position given the meddlesome involvement of Rwanda and Uganda in the country. The government itself has not been forthright in making alliances and advancing strategic positions on crucial matters relating to the conflict because of its innate weaknesses. Indeed, decisions and positions are taken with only short term gains in mind and this has compromised it in the long run.

The people of the DRC want to be rid of foreign rebel troops and all forms of external interference, but lack they the wherewithal to enforce their desires. The weakness of the state and its organs makes it possible for rebel leaders such as Lafontaine to emerge readily. There have been calls within the DRC for decisive action by South Africa and the UN to end the multiple conflicts plaguing the country, but it remains to be seen if this will occur given the rebels well-noted ability to reproduce themselves. It is clearly in the interest of some powerful forces to ensure that the crisis is prolonged given the ill-gotten wealth to be made.

On the whole, Nabudere's work on the conflict in the DRC demonstrates his undeniable concern for the African condition. Here, the orientation is presentist, although he makes a noteworthy discursive maneuver, which is to link the contemporary African condition to the state of the continent during the 1884 Berlin Conference. The mandate at the famous conference was to dismember Africa in accordance with the dictates of the European powers. Under contemporary globalization, the mandate of imperialism has altered. A version of this mandate prescribes the breaking of the continent into mini-states to make it more pliable to the intrusions and devises of global capital. Africa's so-called first world war has truly spectral proportions for having managed to elude the desired degree of global attention.

The intense drive for gold and diamonds, animated solely by a profit motive, treats people only as means to ends. This virtually destroys their humanity to such a degree that real people become nearly invisible in the fray. The gory details of the war, the suffering and deaths of individual human persons, can be ignored while a bewildering assortment of shady financial speculators squabble endlessly over the pluses and minuses of an economic contestation well hidden within the depths of the African jungle.

2

The Concept of Afrikology

The first chapter illustrated how Dani Nabudere's preoccupation with the African condition is demonstrated by his spirited analyses of the crises of the Democratic Republic of Congo (DRC), which bear a contemporary theme. In his later work, he becomes multidisciplinary, or rather, transdisciplinary, and draws more deeply from history. Perhaps it became evident to him that in order to understand the nature and dimensions of African contemporary problems, it is necessary to delve into history in order to avoid merely addressing the symptoms rather than the real causes of the problems. This is one way by which to explain the apparent historical and conceptual disjuncture between a presentist and truly historical approach in Nabudere's explication of the African condition.

Nabudere's presentism bears some qualification in the sense that the event and continuing reverberations of the 1884 Berlin Conference serve as benchmarks by which to understand the African present and its historical continuities: its sordid past, marked as it were, by extreme colonial violence and its present, checkered by more complex and subtle modes of imperialist oppression. Nabudere's work on the Great Lakes Region directly points to these historical continuities and ruptures. These direct inferences grant his analyses a greater depth than they would have had otherwise.

In the present chapter, discussions of Nabudere's concept of Afrikology are undertaken. In discursive terms, Nabudere's focus on the concept immediately connects him with a major strand of Afrocentric thought. In this regard, it will be interesting to observe the ways in which a debate regarding the originality of his thought might play out.

Nabudere begins by citing Charles Taylor on the supposed crisis of Western epistemology which, he argues, had been created by its failure to take into account the reality of intersubjectivity within culture. The consequences of this failure, in his view, have been quite disruptive in causing multiple forms of alienation and the collapse of civility that are evident in dysfunctional societies. If Taylor has been able to identify the fundamentals of the problem, Nabudere, for his part, claims to have the panacea in the concept of Afrikology.

Nabudere goes even further into history, turning to ancient Greek philosophy, in this case, the traditions of thought established by Plato and Aristotle. This supposed fundamental crisis in Western thought has in turn led to a fragmentation of both personal and collective consciousness. To restore the unity of being and consciousness, Nabudere argues that the adoption of the concept of Afrikology is necessary. In his words:

> Afrikology seeks to retrace the evolution of knowledge and wisdom from its source to the current epistemologies, and to try and situate them in their historical and cultural contexts, especially with a view to establishing a new science for generating and accessing knowledge for sustainable use. (2011, 4)

Nabudere ascribes the beginnings of human civilization to the ancient Ethiopians, who in turn, went on to influence the ancient Egyptians in terms of establishing a pantheon of gods and the modes worship associated with the deities. Diodorus of Sicily is named as an authority on the ancient Ethiopians. Gerald Massey is also cited an expert on Egyptology; he argued that the ancient Egyptians discovered "a basis for knowledge generation" (ibid., 5) and the use of sign language.

Massey is credited with claiming that primordial archetypes originated from "inner Africa." These archetypes include Earth as the source of all existence and Darkness as the awesome Devourer. Massey further claims that these ancient mythologies and archetypes, as described by Carl Jung, migrated into Western culture. These mythologies and archetypes, in turn, are to be found within the entire gamut of human culture as opposed to being indigenous to a particular race, ethnicity, or geography. As such, Asians and Europeans merely appropriated forms of knowledge and traditions of astronomy prevalent in ancient Egypt.

Nabudere points out the groundbreaking impact of Egyptian hieroglyphics as being the essential back story for European and Asian myths, legends, and fairytales. Aryan philologists did not have the appropriate knowledge to unearth the connections between the Egyptian hieroglyphic script and the European appropriation of them. This failing created a blind spot in the Western conception and generation of knowledge. As such, it resulted in the tendency for the Western mindset, to individualize the perception of natural phenomena. Nabudere re-reads Jung's work on the formation of archetypes and supports the view that they were first conceived in the hinterlands of Africa before they found their way into ancient Egypt and then eventually to other parts of the world. In several instances, Nabudere makes this sort of claim; that is, many cultural and symbolic representations found in Egypt were, in fact, created in the hinterlands of Africa.

Jung had a contrary reading of the ancient Egyptian world to those of typical Western Egyptologists. He was of the view that in order to understand the Western notion of the "collective unconscious," Western scholars had to look toward Egypt and other parts of Africa. The founding elements of the Western psychoanalytic text, such as ceremonies of rebirth, the pantheon of gods, divine animals, ancient myths and symbols, the sanctification of the tomb, the wonders of the pyramids, elaborate burial rites, and the entire spectrum of the Egyptian collective unconscious are all dimensions of the Egyptian accomplishment that Jung deeply respected. Indeed, the Egyptian civilization, which lasted for two thousand years, provides the basis for understanding just how complex human societies can be.

In ancient Egypt, there occurred a quest never before experienced by humanity to establish a new approach to knowledge, creation, and generation. Pharoah Shabaka, of the twenty-fifth dynasty (770–657 BCE), carried out what has been termed a "re-memorization" of the past by appropriating and codifying ancient Memphite traditions, a project that eventually resulted in the Memphite Theology. In a related vein, Memphis was adopted as the capital of Egypt as well as the site of a thorough-going cultural renaissance. The restoration of Memphis as the capital of ancient Egypt carried far-reaching connotations. It sought to establish Egypt as the Cradle of Civilization apart from having profound architectural, intellectual, as well as religious implications.

Nabudere also explains how the fundamental differences between Western and African epistemologies occurred. In ancient Egypt, the creation of the universe is attributed to Ptah, who was self-created. In addition, Ptah is responsible for the creation of other gods. However, in the cosmology of ancient Greece, to which the West draws much of its inspiration for its epistemological foundations, the cosmos was created out of the pendulum between being and nothingness. Herein lays the telling difference between ancient Egypt and ancient Greece. Greek philosophers such as Plato, through the Theory of Forms, instituted an abstract kind of thinking that did not quite exist in the more holistic ancient Egyptian approach to knowledge generation. Under the influence of Plato, a dichotomization of perception in relation to natural phenomena occurred, that is, a separation between things and forms, or, between the written sign and the thing itself. This epistemic separation led to much of the sort of dialectical thought to be found in Western philosophy.

In ancient Egypt, after the creation of the universe by Ptah, Thoth (or Tehuti) the Egyptian god of the tongue, created the hieroglyphic script and in so doing, developed an intimate relationship between the tongue and heart. In other words, thought springs from the human heart and the tongue articulates what the heart thinks. Here, no binarization of natural phenomena occurs as in Western dialectical thinking, instead a wholeness in thought and enunciation is maintained and it is on this basis that Nabudere advances his philosophy of Afrikology, which is not merely a re-memorization of ancient Egyptian past, but also a program for a sustainable basis for knowledge generation in the contemporary world.

Much of the above can be found in Nabudere's work *Afrikology, Philosophy and Wholeness: An Epistemology* (2011). In what follows, I will give a much closer and detailed reading of the text in order to (1) give some idea as to the viability of Afrikology as an epistemological approach; (2) to situate Nabudere's work within a tradition of similar African epistemologies; and (3) generally to provide an outline by which to interrogate the strengths and weaknesses of Nabudere's propositions.

Nabudere's cites Charles Taylor in alluding to the current malaise within epistemology. This, in turn, has placed contemporary society under tremendous stress as evinced in disturbing forms of alienation, violence, and fragmentation. The dissolution of epistemology can be traced back to the misrepresentation and misunderstanding of ancient Egyptian civilization by scholars of ancient Greece. Nabudere urges a return to the initial locus of the misunderstanding and this proposition forms a key component of his notion of Afrikology. Apart from its role as an epistemological construct, Afrikology is also meant to provide a therapeutic function in healing chronic societal dysfunction and fragmentation. Hence, rather than perceiving knowledge through a materialist lens, it needs instead to be viewed as serving an unambiguous cultural and spiritual role. Nabudere constantly stresses the point that most of the cultural traits or archetypes we commonly associate with ancient Egypt, such as the cult of gods, the offering of sacrifices, and the place of divinity in everyday life can, in fact, be traced to ancient Ethiopia.

Carl Jung explains that in order to understand his definition of what he calls "the collective unconscious," which he claims is manifest within the entire spectrum of humanity, we only need to turn to the archetypes of ancient Egypt such as "the divine kingship, the festival of renewal, the gods, the divine animals, the symbolism of the tomb, the evolution of burial customs, the Temple, the ancient Egyptian psyche and experiences of the species, the pyramids and the texts in the Temples" (ibid., 10). However, some Eurocentric Egyptologists have sought to undermine the position of ancient Egypt as the Cradle of Humankind. Instead, they attempt to push Asia into greater prominence.

External factors – the intervention of foreign forces – also sought to undermine ancient Egypt as prime locus of archetypes until the Twenty-fifth Dynasty pharoah Nefkare Shabaka, of the Kushite (Nubian and Ethiopian) dynasty, instigated what is regarded as the first African renaissance. The renaissance centered on the cosmological system developed at Memphis, during the time it was the capital city of the ancient pharohs of Egypt. It was committed to stone by the order of Shabaka. The Shabaka Text (c. 710 BCE), which was intended to preserve "a work of the ancestors," is alternatively known as The Memphite Theology, and based upon the generative power of God's thought and speech. As with all the Egyptian theologies, the Memphite religion was also political, justifying the primary status of the new capital. The Shabaka Text is perhaps the earliest record of theistic creation in existence. (While the original stone has been lost, the whole Memphite cosmology is preserved on a slab of basalt now exhibited in the Egyptian Sculpture Gallery.) This period is equated with the birth of consciousness, the beginning of the notion of political organization, and the re-memorization of the past.

In this elaborate project of cultural retrieval, it was rediscovered and re-affirmed that "Ptah, the primordial deity, is self-created and is also a creator of the other gods. He is ... the ruler over the unified Kingdom and King of Lower and Upper Egypt and its renewed unification in the hands of Horus. Thus, for the Egyptians, unlike the Greeks, the Cosmos was not suspended between nothing and nothingness, nor did it emerge from nothingness. It was a self-created universe from the oneness that was continuous (ibid., 18).

It is from this primal context that the question of knowledge and its generation and dissemination ought to be understood. The episteme of ancient Egypt made no distinction between the mind and the body. Instead, knowledge and language were perceived as corporeal phenomena. The heart formulates a concept or unit of knowledge, which it then releases to the tongue for proclamation.

In ancient Egypt, the question of knowledge generation involved both conceptual and phonetic dimensions. Written signs represented precisely what they were supposed to. However, in ancient Greece, things and what they represented (forms) were distinct – hence the introduction of abstract dialectical thought in the Greek episteme. It is also believed that, in addition to being the ancient Egyptian god of tongue and creator of hieroglyphics, Thoth was, in fact a human being with mystical properties. Thoth was subsequently appropriated by both the Greeks and Romans and named after their own gods. In Greece he was called Hermes, son of Zeus, the foremost messenger of the gods and the god of oratory.

The Romans referred to Thoth as Hermes Trismergitus, which meant "'Hermes the thrice great,' 'the great one,' 'the greatest,' 'the Master of Masters,' 'the author of astrology, magic, and alchemy'" (ibid., 22). Thoth is ascribed the invention of writing, medicine, chemistry, law, rhetoric, applied mathematics, astronomy, astrology and metaphysics. In addition, he is credited to have written 1,100 books and published 20,000 works in various fields of intellection. However this prodigious intellectual production is devoid of individualism and is instead a product of the collective knowledge amassed by ancient Africans. Hermeneutics, which is the practice of interpreting a variety of texts, is also associated with Thoth. Being a messenger who operates within the divide between men and gods, Thoth was deemed a skillful interpreter of messages.

The art of interpretation is also central to the practices of chicanery, which attempt to go:

beyond the traditional culture and the limits of divination itself by using hermeneutics to interpret these practices and ideas connected with them. Hermeneutic intervention here includes not only the interpretation of recorded historical consciousness, but also the interpretive process to enter the realm of 'symbolic interpretation' and 'double-thinking,' which... is a mode of 'shifting yet discriminating definitions and fluid associations that underlie the Chicane practice (ibid., 47–48).

Individualism in intellectual fields such alchemical studies began with the Greeks, which provides a contrast to African forms of orality, where individualized authorship continues to be somewhat foreign. As Nabudere reminds us, a Kiganda proverb of modern Uganda states, *"amagezi ssi goomu,"* which means knowledge (wisdom) is not the property of a single individual (ibid., 24).

Scholars such as Samir Amin have claimed Plato misunderstood the knowledge systems of ancient Egypt and developed processes of thought based solely on reason. Aristotle, for his part, developed a classificatory grid based on the Platonic model. It has been propounded that Plato's *Republic* is an Athenian reformulation of Egyptian caste system (Vasina 2001, 228). This reformulation had profound consequences in the history of epistemology. As such it has been noted:

> Greek philosophers such as Plato and Aristotle are correctly blamed for having created a false hierarchisation of principles arising out of their search for 'perfect' knowledge due to their inadequate experiences in Egypt. Plato, in particular, is blamed for having created a hierarchisation and distinction between ideas, or *forms* and *things*, and between *outside* and *inside* of things – and hence between virtue and knowledge. From now on in the Greek understanding, the thing and its *form* (the idea) were no longer organically linked (Nabudere 2011: 27).

This, in turn, led to the binarization of epistemic phenomena and hence the dichotomy between appearance and reality, the conditioned and the unconditioned, the absolute and the relative, the subject and the object, etc. This epistemic development is often traced back to Plato, who misread the Memphite Theology in constructing the foundations of Greek philosophy, thus providing the essential impetus for Western thought as a whole. According to Nabudere, this dual mode of reflection, in which the thing is separate from the ideal, is known as the dialectic.

The Greek misrepresentation of ancient Egyptian systems of thought was not itself a wholesale rejection of those systems. Indeed, Cheikh Anta Diop (1991) has argued that Greek philosophy is drawn primarily from Egyptian cosmologies. For instance, the Greek philosophical concept "logos" (whose employment is attributed to Heraclitus and Plato, but actually originates from the ancient Nubian word Ra). With Diop, Nabudere argues that the fragmentation of knowledge forms can only be reversed only if the momentum and dominance of Platonian-Cartesian epistemology cease. A number of times, Nabudere mentions the work of the Copenhagen school of quantum mechanics with its admission of multiple conceptions of reality as a way out of the impasse inherent in the Western epistemological model. As such, a transdisciplinary conception of reality, encompassing the gains of quantum mechanics, is also recommended as an alternative to Cartesian epistemic culture.

Nabudere also argues that the practices of divination and shamanism espouse a transdisciplinarity capable of not only improving but also transforming contemporary epistemology. Shamanism is present in many cultures, but in contemporary times, it is commonly associated with religion or quasi-religious rites, even though shamanic practices had, in the past, been associated with immunology and psychobiology. We are to appreciate:

> the shaman operates by using techniques of ecstasy and the power to leave his body at will during a trancelike state. In cultures where shamanism occurs, sickness is usually thought of as a soul loss and it is thus the shaman's task to enter the spirit world, capture the soul and reintegrate it in the body. A person becomes a shaman either by inheritance or self-election. Thus, in shamanism or divination, there are no boundaries between the spirit, the mind or the body (ibid., 40).

Shamanism is based merely on religious faith but carries within it an elaborate epistemological system that has deep and ancient foundations in human existence itself. Barbara Tedlock captures what being a shaman entails:

> At the heart of shamanic practice is the active pursuit of knowledge. This takes many forms: through calendarial study, divination and prophecy Shamans seek knowledge of the future; and through recitations of myths, epics, charms, spells, songs and the genealogies of previous Shamans, they pass along knowledge of the past and of the spirit world. And since Shamans everywhere seek to know more than they have experienced in their everyday waking lives, they may extend their wisdom through dream journeys that provide a thousand years of human living into a single day. (cited in Nabudere 2011: 43)

Shamans as such do not conform to the accepted linearity of time; they strive to meld with universal consciousness. They are believed to possess the powers to control random events, heal the ill, cure stress and anxiety, and bring about healthy community relations. These general therapeutic functions lead to wholesome deliberations within the community and reduce instances of despondency, psychic tumult, and alienation.

Widespread social fragmentation is believed to have been caused by the fundamental divide that exists between the mind and the body in Western culture and the reluctance or inability to conceive the spirit world as being embedded within the condition of the human (ibid., 45). Disciplines such postcolonial theory emphasize the presence of multiple knowledge forms and traditions as opposed to mainstream Western scholarship, which tends to view such repressed forms as being relativist and essentialist.

Just as to be found in practices of chicanery, Nabudere states that the shaman is thought to possess a double personality just as a trickster has. In addition, a duality of consciousness straddles both the material and the immaterial worlds. The resilience of the trickster tradition was evident in the slave plantations of the New World, where captive slaves were able to find solace in sorcery, magic, mystical invocations, and the enchantment of the spirit world in the face of the daily brutalities of slave existence. Through the agency of memory, the inversions of mimicry, and the invocations of the spirit world, slaves on American plantations were not only able to establish and maintain some degree of psychic equilibrium, but perhaps more importantly, were able to create modern African-American culture as we know it. Furthermore, this resistance against Western hegemony formed the basis for the emergence and development for the ideology of pan-Africanism.

There are reasons to believe that shamanism is making its way into hegemonic cultural contexts through sometimes remarkable means. Harry Smith, an American archivist, artist, and experimental filmmaker was commissioned by a record label – Folkways – to produce an anthology of American folk music, which would otherwise have been lost in the frenzy and sheer destruction of the World War II. Smith delivered eighty-four songs along a system of ordering based on ancient Egyptian cosmology. Ballads were classified as green/water, social music came under the heading red/fire, and songs as blue/air. The cover art carried a seventeenth century engraving of the celestial monochord, which represented Pythagorean music theory. Smith's archivist mind also organized his anthology using ideas drawn from hermetic philosophy. Eventually, a cult grew around Smith's anthology that went on to influence the folk boom in the United States during the 1960s, producing figures such as Bob Dylan, Joan Baez, Jerry Garcia, and others. In this way, Smith's work found its way into influential artistic circles and most especially the American counterculture.

Ancient rock art reveals much about shamanism. Formerly, Western interpretations of ancient African rock art state that the forms evident in the practice were, in fact, stylized human beings. However, recent research ascribes the forms in rock art to hallucinatory experiences of shamans as opposed to being literal representations of the material world. Apart from being representations of hallucinatory and spiritual states, rock art contain 'the shamanic roots of modern religion" (ibid., 60).

Shamans of advanced age who were unable to endure the rigors of all night long sessions in trance have accomplished states of heightened consciousness with the aid of the hallucinogenic mushrooms, psilocybin. Shamans' trancelike states are akin to spiritual journeys, duing which shamans consult with deities and the departed on behalf of their communities. They then return to the material world with renewed psychic energies, with which they are alleged to heal the infirm, restore communal harmony, and bring random elements under control.

One of Nabudere's central arguments is that African cosmologies and epistemologies can be harnessed within the context of postmodernity for a new cultural synthesis as a panacea for the current existential malaise that afflicts the contemporary period. He further states that if recourse to the cultural accomplishments of ancient Greece has been possible, the same should be true about ancient inner Africa. In his view, postmodern rationality has failed and in order to address this failure, an existential symbiosis between humankind and nature would have to be engendered as it happened in pre-Athenian times. Under the Greek epistemological model, abstract rationality as the basis for the construction of knowledge and experience has been undervalued. Kant's *Critique of Pure Reason* is a continuation of the Greek model which found acolytes in Johann G. Fichte, Friedrich Schelling, Friedrich Schleiermacher, and G. W. F. Hegel. But this model is now being challenged by advances in quantum mechanics, which are highlighting the interconnectedness between humankind and nature. Nabudere argues that there are fallacies in Western traditions of rationality stemming from Plato's misunderstanding ancient Egyptian cosmologies:

> It follows that the Greeks' attempt to philosophise without an adequate understanding of Egyptian sources was bound to be misleading to their successors. Since their lack of understanding of the source of knowledge in its origin was fatal in their own context, it was also bound to pass on the weaknesses to their European successors. This is made clearer when referring to Diop's reflection on the Greeks' emulation of the African philosophy. Indeed, as Diop has demonstrated, the Greek scholars had embraced ancient Egyptian wisdom, but later abstracted aspects of that knowledge to develop their own system of 'reasoning' as... in the case of Plato (ibid., 76).

The Greek dialectical method draws from the cosmological forms of inner Africa, in which creation is believed to founded on a dual mode. Ra, the Egyptian deity is believed to have created the divine pairs: Shu and Tefnut, and Geb and Nut. In this combination we find the four elements (air, water, earth, and fire) that are central in the corpus of the Presocratic philosophers: Thales of Miletus, Anaximander, Heraclitus, Parmenides, and Anaxagoras. The original African model that provided the basis for this also occurs in pairs: Osiris and Isis, Seth and Nephthys.

Having criticized the epistemological tradition developed by Platonian-Cartesian-Kantian thought for causing much of the fragmentation and alienation in the contemporary world, Nabudere urges a return to an ethos of Nubian interconnectedness. He is aware that this project of cultural retrieval would be an arduous task: "a return to the ancient Egyptian or 'inner Africa' system of ancient times is not possible in its pure form" (ibid., 71).

The Platonian-Cartesian-Kantian model on which much of Western thought is based, in Nabudere's view, is deeply flawed and in order to overcome its shortcomings and to discern the antecedents of the crisis of contemporary reason, we are urged to return to the being of language. In this particular instance, the languages of Africa are offered as a beacon that possesses the wholeness and interconnectedness inherent in Presocratic existential relations and epistemic frameworks. Scholars of inner Africa believed that the heart is the locus of reason, but Platonian epistemology separated things from their forms, a dialectical method of reasoning then emerged and created a profound division between humankind and nature thereby leading to chronic fragmentation, the sterility of dialectical thinking, meaningless hierarchization, and epistemic absolutism.

Not all of Nabudere's proposals about the return to an ethos of wholeness and interconnectedness are convincing. He suggests the employment of African languages as a possible way of attaining that goal, but has very little to say about the logistic requirements involved in such a project:

> It follows... that it is through languages and traditions based on those languages that humanity can dialogue with one another and come to a consensus about a new future. Hence, the recognition and development of African languages through which the overwhelming masses of the African people are able to communicate are the preconditions for bringing about a true human understanding and discourse with other cultures and civilizations (ibid., 90).

Obviously, this proposition involves numerous daunting practical concerns about which Nabudere is silent. For instance, he needs to address the issue of which African language, for example, Hausa, Swahili, Yoruba, or Wolof, is most appropriate for this type of conceptual undertaking. Also, we need more evidence on the ravages of "the paradigm of oppositionality" (103), as Nabudere terms the crisis of Western epistemology- on which most of the contemporary traditions of rationality are based.

But there is a progressive element within Nabudere's work. Once again, he re-affirms invaluable contributions of scholars such as Diop and Théophile Obenga, whose problematizations and interrogations of origins of African thought systems have demonstrated that there is much depth to discovered in those traditions. When this approach is juxtaposed along the work of African philosophers such as Peter O. Bodunrin, a superficiality and artificiality become evident in the latter's thought. African philosophers of the analytic school adopted wholesale the Cartesian model of analysis, thereby contributing to the excesses of dialectical thought.

For his part, Nabudere believes the hermeneutic approach can lead to "the recovery of [African] knowledge" as well as constitute an antidote to the paradigm of oppositionality, in which most of the canons of rationality are mired. Also by adopting a hermeneutic approach, the centrality of Thoth as an interpreter of mystical messages is again brought to the fore just as the value of shamanic and trickster traditions is re-asserted. In Nabudere's view, the repressed histories of those traditions are likely to enrich the common fount of our humanity.

African discourses on Egyptology are becoming increasingly more established. They often seek to counter the common Eurocentric bias that holds that Africa has no history or culture worth talking about. African scholars of Egyptology, in addition to some North Atlantic intellectuals, are now claiming that Africa is, in fact, the Cradle of Humankind and hence, the foremost vehicle of civilization. Increasingly, research is deepening in this respect. But Nabudere is taking the project even further.

Rather than stop with what he considers to be proof of the primacy of the Egyptian past and its numerous cultural and scientific achievements, Nabudere suggests attempts should be made to connect that illustrious past with the African present. This, remarkably, is what makes his project worthy of careful attention, and this is essentially what his philosophy of Afrikology is about: tracing the historical, cultural, scientific, and social links between the Cradle of Humankind and the contemporary world with a view to healing the seismic severances occasioned by violence, false thinking, war, loss, and dispossession to accomplish an epistemological and psychic sense of wholeness for African collective self. Of course, this proposition has considerable importance as a philosophy of universalism and not just as an African project. Afrikology intends to transcend the dichotomies inherited from Western epistemology (and culture as whole) that maintain a divide between mind and body or heart and mind and revert instead to an earlier conceptual tradition perfected in ancient Egypt that conceives of knowledge generation as a holistic enterprise, where the fundamental binarisms of the Western universe do not really apply.

Nabudere's work does not only foreground the significance of Egypt as a cultural fountainhead. Other parts of Africa, such as Ethiopia, contributed to the eventual flowering of Egypt as a beacon of civilization. The common ancient practices of worshipping kings as gods, establishing and maintaining pantheons of gods, and elaborate ceremonies for the dead are all practices that first began in Ethiopia, and which were carried on by the ancient Egyptians. Also, sign language, in existence in the hinterlands of Africa such as among the Pygmies and the Khoi-San of Southern Africa, parallels or even predates the representations of totemism, fetishism, and Egyptian hieroglyphics.

3

Further Explorations in Afrikology

Dani Nabudere's monograph, *Afrikology and Transdisciplinarity: A Restorative Epistemology* (2012) adopts a somewhat different approach from that of *Afrikology, Philosophy, and Wholeness*. It is a product of a research project conducted under the auspices of the Marcus Garvey Pan-African Institute, Mbale, which he helped found. In addition, the project resulted in an international conference with the title, "Restorative Justice and its Relationship to International Humanitarian Law," held in Nairobi, 2008, with delegates from Uganda, Kenya, Tanzania, Rwanda, and Southern Sudan. Within the context of this project, Nabudere attempts to establish a connection between restorative justice and Afrikology. His methodological approach is essentially transdisciplinary; it rejects the traditional divisions between academic disciplines while advocating a more holistic strategy toward knowledge production.

Nabudere posits that knowledge itself emanates from the heart, which processes the sensations and experiences derived from the five senses. The *word* is the vehicle through which knowledge is transmitted and human communities function on the basis of the correlation between themselves, language, and reason. At this juncture, Nabudere introduces another element – cosmology – that distances him from the Western paradigm. According to him, humankind is inextricably connected to the cosmos, which not only provides the rationale for knowledge generation, but goes on to structure such knowledge in a holistic manner. Holism connects social, cultural, political, and spiritual dimensions of knowledge into a seamless whole, something that had been long discarded by Athenian rationality.

Similarly, Nabudere is of the view that justice can only make sense if it stems from the lived experiences of the people(s) concerned and if it acts a glue between disparate cultures. In this way, the greatest possible understanding can be derived. Justice, as such, should not be conceived and implemented as a rigid set of societal injunctions to punish infringements upon the law in a manner that is removed from the pulse, aspirations, and failings of society. Restoration and reparations, it is argued, are also vital to a holistic understanding of justice. Accordingly:

restoration in this sense then seemed to have a deeper meaning than 'justice' as understood in the Roman Statute. It became a philosophic restatement of the need for a broader understanding of the holistic relationships between human beings, the perceptions and conceptions of reality, and the institutional frameworks in which these relationships are understood and practiced. (ibid., 2)

If this conception of justice incorporating restoration and reparation is adopted, society would, in turn, become more inhabitable and consequently less conflictual. The ideal to aim for is to strive to establish a human community based on cordiality, mutuality, and solidarity, which is a far cry from one based on discord, destructive competition, and the exercise of transgressive power. Again, Nabudere faults age-long Western conceptual schemes and methodologies for the entrenched binarization of collective modes of perception, analyses, and organization, which, in turn, have skewed the possibilities for developing holistic societies. This is a train of thought he pursues consistently in both *Afrikology, Philosophy, and Wholeness* and in *Afrikology and Transdisciplinarity*. Taken together, these two works constitute a summa of his late theoretical preoccupations.

Western philosophical thought, beginning from Plato up to contemporary times, has refuted what Nabudere deems the inherent unities and complementarities of basic human society. In order to redress the violence and chaos resulting from that outcome, the current task would be to evolve alternative epistemologies that are more representative of both humanity and nature. As such, much of the conflict in northern Uganda can be ascribed to the failure to address the crucial issues of the conflict in a holistic fashion.

Nabudere then criticizes John Rawls's *Theory of Justice* (1971), which in his view, fails to see that social and economic inequalities in societies may constitute a kind of injustice by themselves. Furthermore, the same detrimental compartmentalizaton that characteristizes post-Hellenic human society undermines the efficacy of Rawls' conception of justice. As human society generally lacks fundamental unity and complementarity, virtually all the institutions, traditions, and practices to be found in it are severely fragmented.

To cope with the problems and challenges of human society, multidisciplinary and interdisciplinary models of problem-solving have been advanced. Nabudere goes a step further to advocate a transdisciplinary approach encompassing as many multidisciplinary perspectives as possible. Society can become more manageable and equitable if the monopoly of power and violence enjoyed by the state is relinquished. Nabudere argues that the contemporary democratic state is no different from feudal regimes in the manner in which it controls and determines the nature of violence.

The administration of justice, accordingly, should be the prerogative of as many stakeholders as possible to be truly fair and representative. At the conceptual level, the dichotomy between "retributive" and "redistributive" justice needs to be addressed to arrive at more holistic outcomes. The adversarial, or retributive, system of justice relies on the skill of advocates to manipulate the spirit of law to sway the judge or jury to secure favorable outcomes for their clients.

The inquisitorial mode of justice obtains in continental Europe where judges are empowered to investigate a legal case until they arrive at whatever findings they deem fit. However, since the period these two distinct systems of justice became established, society has become even more complex as a result of the more intricate evolution of civil society, the erosion of the powers of the state, and finally, the emergence of non-statist actors and formations that are able to operate at a transnational level, which often bypass and in some cases undermine an already enfeebled nation-state. This kind of scenario has led to yet another plane of dichotomization between international law and its transnational beneficiaries on the one hand, and the often invisible subjects of domestic law on the other. The emergence of terrorism on a global scale has led to the remodeling of relations between states and new modalities pertaining to the spread and maintenance of global security.

These various contradictions at the conceptual level reverberate right down to the local level, most especially in African societies where there is a continuing tussle between tradition and modernity, which, in turn, affects the composition of institutions and the modes of governance. Oftentimes, there are indigenous perceptions and expectations of justice that have very little to do with postcolonial Western-inflected conceptions. Nabudere points out that these mismatched conceptions have caused a lack of clarity regarding how to deal with the atrocities and human rights abuses committed by members of the Lord's Resistance Army and the Uganda Peoples Defence Force in Uganda. In a related situation, the tradition-versus-modernity problematic in Africa, in which Western powers such as the United States privileged modernity over indigenous cosmologies, has created the most unseemly scenarios characterized by numerous failed states and skewed experiments in democracy and modernity. In addition, it has also resulted in horrific despotic regimes, which are sometimes supported by the same Western nations supposedly intent on exporting democracy.

In order to adopt a comprehensive understanding of societal stability, several variables are involved that include:

> economic security, health security, environmental security, personal security, food security, community security, political security and other related rights such as freedom from fear and freedom from want (Nabudere 2012: 17).

Nabudere goes on to condemn unduly centralized forms of government in Africa because the over-centralization of power by African countries is glaringly plagued by a variety of woes ranging from inefficiency, the constant threat of dismemberment, and finally, the outright collapse of the state. Nabudere is of the view that the devolution of power is a helpful way of confronting these issues.

In the final analysis, the proper functioning of global systems, international legal frameworks, and consequently the emerging global civil society would be greatly enhanced by incorporating local requirements and considerations.

Fragmentation, atomization, dissociation, and extreme individualism are all phenomena that Nabudere continues to decry as the causes for the chronic disharmony in human society. In addition, Cartesian analysis is responsible for the largely irreconcilable split between mind and body. Academic scholarship went on to entrench the fragmentation by which many disparate disciplines emerged and continue to emerge without interdisciplinary let alone transdisciplinary considerations. The present state of human consciousness has, in turn, been adversely affected by this persistent and pervasive fragmentation within collective and institutional memory. Western and modern epistemology generally have not only ended in severe disharmony against which Nabudere rails, but also in the current crisis of capitalism to which there appears to be no panacea. A transdisciplinary consciousness is required, in Nabudere's opinion, to return human society to a considerably more wholesome state.

Nabudere holds the view that a primal link connects humankind, vegetation, the animal world, and the galaxy, which Cartesian rationality and scientific knowledge have ruptured. He therefore urges for a "reconvergence" that would restore a "oneness" to the procedures of knowledge making. This view is repeatedly stressed without a concurrent proffering of the modalities by which this objective is to be accomplished. What he does instead is to mention a few scholars who have argued that the pioneers of the Enlightenment caused a radical break in human knowledge by downplaying and, in fact, refuting the uses of religion, divination, and other related forms of mystical cognition in favor of the abstract sciences, which were then applied to the animate and non-animate worlds. This rupture again contributes to the problems faced by contemporary society.

Yet advocates of the abstract sciences – and they are in the majority – argue that all problems are solvable through them while non-scientific varieties of cognition are suspect since they are regarded as superstition, dogma, heresy, or conjecture. Non- scientific modes of cognition, it was deemed, was often the preserve of the powerful and the cunning, who were able to dominate and exploit the weak, gullible, and intellectually deficient. Science and rational thought, on the other hand, served as an antidote to these excesses and abuses in society. Cartesian rationality held that the universe was governed by immutable laws that need to be discovered by scientific experimentation and procedure. In addition, these laws were intersubjective and the procedures could be replicated indefinitely. The Galileo-Cartesian mathematicization of reality eventually led to the dominance of science to the detriment of non-scientific variants of knowledge.

However, as Giambattista Vico has pointed out (1968), science is just a human invention, and therefore liable to the errors that usually plagued such human endeavors. Human cultures and societies, he argued, thrive on the modes of knowledge they are able to evolve through language and indigenous systems of thought. In advancing this line of argument, Vico provided the foundations for the disciplines of cultural anthropology, comparative linguistics, art criticism, and comparative mythology. But a powerful contrary trend emerged in the form of Newtonian science, which sought to apply the gains of scientific rationality and procedures to the obviously non-scientific domains of ethics, politics, and interpersonal relations, in other words, in the often hazy, nondescript world of human society.

The natural sciences were often uncreatively applied to the purview of the social sciences without taking into consideration that the former do have real limitations as to their scope of applicability. This maneuver resulted in what in philosophical vocabulary is termed an error of categorization. In addition, both domains of knowledge mimicked each other rather than seek out genuine complementarities. The unquestioned faith in science eventually led to what may be termed the discourses of predictability in the form of the emergence of "future studies," "visions" and "scenario-building" exercises all of which in turn paved the way for a more widespread acknowledgement and appreciation of non-linearity as being considerably reflective of a significant proportion of reality.

Hermeneutics, is a branch of knowledge that deals with interpretation, especially of the Bible or literary texts, advanced by Western scholars to deal with the problem of exegesis. These arts of interpretation and textual recuperation can be traced back to the ancient Egyptian god, Thoth (or Tehuti), who, in Roman mythology is called Hermes Trismegistus. In ancient Greek cosmology, this deity was responsible for conveying messages between the realm of the living and the gods. Hermes, as such, was tasked the interpretation of messages, which made him a custodian and dispenser of esoteric knowledge.

Martin Heidegger repositioned the significance of hermeneutics as a vital procedure for knowledge generation. He argued that the world could not be comprehended by the accumulation of undigested facts and snippets of information and that a philosophy of interpretation was required to generate and establish meaning. The hermeneutic quest largely seeks to address the lapses of the natural sciences by introducing the value of transdisciplinarity. Cartesian rationality, so Nabudere claims, is characterized by epistemological dualisms and hierarchies that splinter and dichotomize the field of knowledge in the broadest sense, while transdisciplinarity mediated by hermeneutics provides the panacea. Nabudere also calls attention to the Kuhnian view of science as an endeavor marked by sudden and often unexpected shifts in tradition and hegemony. Nabudere then launches an almost unprecedented attack on the entire edifice of modern knowledge:

> For this transdisciplinary approach to knowledge production to be useful, we
> have to find much deeper ways in which we can reconnect with the ancient sense

of wholeness as created by the ancient Africans, but which were fabricated by the Greeks, among others. Plato and Aristotle are a small part of the problem, although their philosophic approaches were broader than those adopted by European scholars and philosophers who narrowed the horizons of knowledge through Cartesian fragmented academic scientific method. Quite clearly they laid the ground for the philosophical and metaphilosophical manipulations, but the Jewish and European fabrication of ancient Egypt's achievements have been even more ominous and dangerous (Nabudere 2012: 32).

Nabudere then reminds us that in the *The African Origin of Civilization: Myth and Reality* (1974), Cheikh Anta Diop advocated for a more comprehensive and integrated approach to knowledge making. Similarly, Basarab Nicolescu has decried the continuing fragmentation of knowledge under the onslaught the specialization and multiplication of academic disciplines which are increasingly distant and disconnected from each other (ibid.,33). The phenomenon of fragmentation can be discerned beyond the field of knowledge where the whole world exists as a disjointed agglomeration of countries, regions, and various geographical units further splintered by the realities of race, religion, class, ethnicity, gender, and sexuality. Individuals can be a jumbled presence of paranoia, psychoses, and neuroses, markedly disconnected from both self and society.

Accordingly, some scholars have advocated a new collective philosophy, in nutshell, nothing short of a new kind of consciousness that would mend the legacy and ravages of fragmentation and the age-long epistemological impasse. To account for the totality of existence, Nabudere agrees with Nicolescu that transdisciplinarity is the most appropriate way to transcend the chronic limitations of monodiscplinarity, multidisciplinarity, and interdisciplinarity. Accordingly, reality is filtered through a multidimensional lens as opposed to being fractured as if through a prism. African cosmologies, on the other hand, in Nabudere's view, reflect the uni-dimensionality of reality. Nabudere identifies a convergence between the ideas of Nicolescu and Diop attesting to the multi-referentiality of existence.

In another vein, conceptual innovations, such as chaos theory, highlight the complexity in science and nature, thereby pointing the way toward more open systems of knowledge. In the realm of nature and culture, effective prognosis is not always possible or accurate in spite of the numerous claims of science to the contrary. According to Nabudere, chaos theory has three far-reaching consequences: first, it questions and places in parenthesis the status of expert knowledge; it undermines the hierarchies that exist in different fields of knowledge; and it re-establishes the hitherto discarded relations between chance and determinism. The linear paradigm advanced by science made far-reaching judgments and forecasts based on trusted notions of rationalism, order, and universalism, which were, in turn, largely adopted by social science in ways that were not always verifiable or could not always be supported. In the realm of politics, the dismemberment of the Soviet Union and the termination of ideological bipolarity resulted in other fissures, spheres of contestation, and scenarios that had not been anticipated. Social science, in failing to predict accurately these unexpected scenarios, appeared to make the adoption of transdisciplinarity more urgent.

The research paradigm incorporating empiricism and conceptual analysis did not convincing deliver the required outcomes despite claims to neutrality and objectivity. Hans-Georg Gadamer also questioned the professed neutrality and objectivity of science, as bias and subjectivity were invariably ingrained within the quest for knowledge (Gadamer and Palmer 2007: 236). A particular research environment or tradition would inevitably privilege specific approaches and methods to the exclusion of others, which would in turn bedevil it with a certain insularity. Hermeneutics, on the other hand, encourages open-endedness as the most viable approach for knowledge generation. Consequently, there is an evident opposition between positivist science and hermeneutics, which is further extended into the disparity between what is termed "soft" and "hard" science. Nabudere constantly stresses the need to adopt a holistic approach to knowledge making. This approach would entail a keen consideration for language, mores, customs, and other related repertoires to be found in a particular culture. The hard sciences would simply tend to ignore this category of variables.

In addition, Nabudere points out that established canons of rationality increasingly become less self-critical and less inquisitive as they become more hegemonic. Apart from arguing for the virtues of hermeneutics, triangulation, which involves a multiplicity of research approaches, has also been advanced by scholars of a serious transdisciplinary bent. Advocates of triangulation have argued that in employing different methods, theoretical approaches, and researchers for a particular knowledge-making process, a comprehensive account is unveiled, which notably encompasses both positivist science and hermeneutics. As such, triangulation is a methodological approach that combines positivistic and hermeneutical practices in generating knowledge. In addition to the need for the benefits of transdisciplinarity, triangulation, and hermeneutics, a considerable degree of reflexivity is required within science to mirror and engage with events occurring within its context. This level of reflection, Nabudere avers, leads to the difference between a "diachronics of knowing" centered on what precisely it is that we know, and a "synchronics of knowing," based on the presentation of the modalities by which we concoct of particular version of reality.

What we are able to know has always been mediated by factors of uncertainty, chaos, and unpredictability. This has enabled a more vigorous questioning of many of the assumptions of science on the part of society at large. In a somewhat related vein, the received universality of science has been unraveled to demonstrate that scientific concepts often work differently in various cultural contexts when mediated by conditions of locality under which they may assume altered connotations. A greater degree of investigation into the interface between science and society founded on self-organizing principles is deemed necessary to strengthen society on the one hand, and to improve the efficacy of science while at the same time deepening its capacities for self-critique on the other. As such, a co-evolutionary ethic involving both science and society is being promoted by scholars such as Nabudere who are advancing a new understanding of transdisciplinarity.

It now being increasingly noted by scholars of transdisciplinarity that all societies, regardless of the levels of technological development, are knowledge-producing, and that different societies pursue and refine various kinds of knowledge depending on their requirements. Multiculturalism appears to have influenced the scientific temperament in the wake of widespread Third World decolonization and the demise of the European imperial project. In the light of these major sociopolitical events, what is required is a co-evolutionary trajectory between science and society. Science was traditionally highly intolerant of supposedly non-scientific and non-Western orders of knowledge, which is increasingly viewed within the current transdisciplinary climate as a source of considerable cognitive impoverishment. Some non-Western cultures and societies such as the Japanese have evolved ways of adapting and modifying their indigenous knowledge traditions to accommodate some of the more palatable gains of science. In this way, they were able to develop the Lean manufacturing model that produced beautiful and efficient automobiles, making the American Fordist model obsolete (see, for example, Shingo 1984).

The mono-functionality of the dominant tradition of science had to acknowledge the uses, aims, and gains of other subsystems that came about as a result of specific cultural practices, norms, methodologies, intellectual traditions, and epistemologies. The interpretation of scientific findings in relation to nature is mediated by language and culture, which invariably creates the need for significant levels of division of intellectual labor. The sociality of knowledge systems is also of vital importance. By this, one means the ways and means by which knowledge adapts, circulates, and gains applicability and legitimacy within a given sociocultural context. When knowledge forms find ready applicability and relevance within a specific culture, it significantly increases the possibilities for broadening their empirical dimension. Dominant science does not readily accept the value of non-hegemonic knowledge systems and this is often decried by mainstream scientists and knowledge workers.

The critique of dominant science, in Nabudere's view, allows for the inclusion of Afrikology as an alternative epistemology, which he says is, "an epistemology of knowledge generation and application that has roots in African cosmology and worldviews" (2012: 78). Ethnocentrism then becomes an inherent ingredient of epistemic propagation. Nabudere believes, with Diop, that The Cradle of Humankind resides in Africa, from which fully formed human beings were said to have emerged. Nabudere also points out that some recent genetic research supports this thesis.

Gadamer is not the only major intellectual figure that had advocated a new orientation within the annals of science. Diop also argued for a greater degree of receptiveness within the natural sciences toward other traditions and procedures of knowledge making that is truly reflective of the holistic and hermeneutic temper. Diop, as known within Afrocentric circles, copiously draws from ancient Egyptian epistemology in affirming the centrality of both the African subject and African cosmology. By extension, Africanity and broadly inclusive epistemology become, under Nabudere's handling, a discursive nexus undergirded by hermeneutics, transdisciplinarity, and Afrikology.

According to Nabudere, the ancient Egyptian intellectual tradition was organized on "insisting on communication and dialogue through the world created by the heart" (ibid., 80). In this sense, Afrikology then becomes a project of epistemic recuperation, drawing its main inspiration from Egyptology and related Afrocentric discourses. Such a project of recuperation immediately admits of a profound severance within the epistemic field. Afrikology and perhaps Afrocentricity generally, holds that contemporary knowledge as a whole is misguided, truncated, and therefore, false as a result of the profound severance Nabudere claims currently exists. Accordingly, this severance can be traced back to the Platonic-Aristotelian paradigm that misapplied the contents, accomplishments, and intentions of ancient Egyptian thought. In *Black Athena* (1987–2006) Martin Bernal claimed that Hermeticism, a product of the thought of the ancient Egyptian god Thoth, was downplayed by both the Western Enlightenment and Christianity because of its competitive standing in relation to the Western canons of rationality.

In spite of the Western repudiation of ancient Egyptian rationality, some of the gains of the tradition have managed to filter into the Western intellectual tradition such as notions pertaining to the sanctity and immortality of the human spirit, the concept of humanism, the interaction between spirit and matter, and the entire notion of eternity as an epistemological construct. Plato had visited ancient Egypt with the aim of learning its thought and mysteries. However, scholars such as Samir Amin (1989) aver that he did not stay long enough to learn about those mysteries and hence privileged reason as the central and perhaps also only component of rationality, which, rather than representing the major canon of ancient Egyptian thought, was, in fact, a misinterpretation and hence a refutation of Egyptian forms of knowledge. It was, as such, a different cosmology.

The Platonic rupture between spirit and matter created an effective discontinuity in what had hitherto being a unified conception of knowledge. Reason ceased to be mediated by spirit and which within the context of modernity, Nabudere claims to be the source of numerous instances of fragmented identities and hence the frenetic quests for the recovery of selfhood and concerted attempts to return spirit to its lost and uncertain place. In ancient Egyptian thought, relativism stood alongside universalism, a crucial distinction which both Socrates and Plato failed to appreciate. The protracted reign of the metanarrative of Western rationality commenced, offering itself as univeralism par excellence. Nabudere claims this universalism shunned the human consciousness in its severance from spirituality.

Nabudere argues that the Western notion of universalism can be both false and incomplete as evident in the so-called crisis of reason, those rationally unresolvable contradictions that reason itself unearths. Reason itself is incomplete and has its severe limitations. Nabudere informs us that German romanticism acknowledges this crisis and seeks to make amends in its concerted critique of materialism. Heidegger announces the repudiation of being as a direct consequence of the crisis (Nabudere 2012: 80). It has been argued that overcoming the impasse of rationality would ultimately lead to the emergence of a higher civilization.

Nabudere argues that the divorce of spirituality from existence, the sacralization of materialism, the denaturing of nature and the secularization – diminution and eventual disappearance – of the spirit that have occurred under the aegis of modernity are the main causes of the crisis of reason. Here, he is pointing out the philosophical error of categorization for the manner in which technology has become accepted as the panacea for all human woes. In order to effect redress, a reconvergence of humanity and nature, spirit and matter, science and non-science is necessary. The hegemony of universalism, materiality, Western science, and rationality must be ruptured to accommodate other less dominant forms of knowledge and understanding.

The impasse of rationality may also be a reflection of the limits of science as a cognitive endeavor. Nabudere advocates a recovery and restoration of discarded forms of knowledge that unquestionably define the meaning of "human." Afrikology and the African concept of "ubuntu," – the self exists in the other and vice versa – Nabudere claims, attest to the underlying indivisibility of the universe, which, if appropriately accommodated and acknowledged, establishes a balance and mutual intelligibility between humanity and nature. The elements of interdependence, interconnectedness, and complementarity are what would account for the balance. Another crucial element Nabudere mentions is "energy," which accounts for the constant evolutionary surge present in the universe, involving both chaos and stability and which has to be mediated by an accompanying growth of knowledge.

Knowledge generation itself is far from being a transparent endeavor. Noam Chomsky (1986) urges for an approach that enables seekers after knowledge to apprehend underlying patterns within often chaotic phenomena, surfaces, and fields. However, in attempting to discern explanatory models for such apparently random phenomena, so-called experts usually narrow down the sites of inquiry into academic specialties, which are often disconnected to other related phenomena and fields of study. Excessive compartmentalization and over-specialization of knowledge have arguably led to a generalized impoverishment of imaginative and intellectual attitudes.

Nabudere draws attention to two considerable problems concerning the question of knowledge raised by Noam Chomsky: Plato's Problem, the name given by Chomsky to "explain how we know so much given that the evidence we have available to us is so sparse" (Chomsky 1986, xxvii) and Orwell's Problem, or, "why we know and understand so little, even though the evidence available to us is so rich" (xxvii). Chomsky asserts:

> In the modern era, ... the doctrines of the state religion are firmly implanted and widely believed, in utter defiance of plain fact, particularly by the intelligentsia who construct and propagate these doctrines, those who take on the task of "manufacture of consent" (Walter Lippman) or "engineering of consent" (Edward Bernays) (ibid.).

In order to solve Orwell's Problem, there is the need "to discover the institutional and other factors that block our insight and understanding in crucial areas of our lives and ask why they are effective" (ibid.). Chomsky continued:

> In the case of Plato's problem, the questions ultimately belong to the sciences ... The problem is to discover explanatory principles, often hidden and abstract, to make some sense of phenomena that seem on the surface chaotic, discordant, laking any meaningful pattern. The study of Orwell's problem is quite different. The patterns that lie behind the most important phenomena of political, economic, and social life are not very difficult to discern, although much effort is devoted toward obscuring the fact; and the explanation for what will be observed by those who can free themselves fro mthe doctrines of the faith is hardly profound or difficult to discover or comprehend. The study of Orwell's problem, then, is primarily a matter of accumulating evidence and examples to illustrate what should be fairly obvious to a rational observer even on superficial inspection, to establish the conclusion that power and privilege function much as any rational mind would expect, and to exhibit the mechanisms that operate to yield the results that we observe (ibid., xxviii).

While addressing Plato's Problem centers on possibilities for critical thought and the unleashing of the imagination, consideration of Orwell's Problem cautions us against the use of dogma and state violence inherent in manufactured dissent, both of which undermine the capacity for independent thought. Just as human thought and imagination can be manipulated and restrained, Thomas Malthus (1798) implied that human beings ought to be also controlled as human population growth will always be greater than a population's ability to sustain itself. As such, Nabudere asserts that unrestrained population growth is likely to lead to "diseases, epidemics, wars, plagues and famines" (2012: 94). Malthus believed that clear economic analysis of human population growth had a link with theodicy. Subsquently, various kinds of political leadership see connections between global peace and security and population statistics. The Foucauldian notion of biopolitics is applicable here, whereby a social body is viewed as an organism that can be policed, manipulated, and subjected to dictates of an overriding power.

Nabudere points out that the United States contemplates its options seriously when deciding whether to aid foreign nations. Rather than starve foreign populations, it prefers to engineer war and conflict to police them. For instance, in 1960, Mobutu Sese Seko of the former Zaire was useful to the US CIA in deposing a constitutionally elected government. Later, when Mobutu was deemed superfluous to US requirements, a war situation was contrived to force him out of power on the one hand, and as a ploy to protect US interests within the country, on the other. By 2003, it is estimated that 1.7 million Zairians had lost their lives in the war that had been created without their consent or complete knowledge.

Ultimately, Nabudere rejects Malthusian analysis because of its perceived unilinearity, which denies subaltern populations the facility of agency. Unilinear thought also fails to consider that social innovation best occurs in contexts that are heterogeneous, fluid, and open-ended. In the same vein, innovative ideas require conducive cultural environments in order to take root and flourish.

Integral innovation seeks to overcome the shortcomings of contemporary social science research, which, in its fixation with rationalism and pragmatism, has become increasingly disconnected with society; in other words it has adopted a reductive orientation rather than a holistic approach. Nabudere argues that not much innovation can occur within the current bent of social science research. Instead, innovation is more likely to take place when there is free interaction among public, private, civic, and environmental sectors of society (ibid., 104). When integral research and innovation are combined positive outcomes can be observed at the individual and collective levels.

Similarly, social constructivism considers the context and culture in which knowledge generation occurs. By extension, the notion of intersubjectivity is based upon the cultural as well as social foundations of constructs of knowledge. As such, "knowledge is derived from interactions between people and their environments and [...] such knowledge resides within cultures" (ibid., 106). Social constructivists are of the view that understandings of reality emerge from specific social and cultural contexts which can be ultimately taken to mean that knowledge is a product of human thought and activity.

Nabudere goes on to add his voice to those in opposition to capitalist ideology. George Soros had pronounced that a "crisis of capitalism" exists (1998). Nabudere stresses that economic analysts found it difficult to explain the full dimensions of the crisis (especially after the 2008 global economic meltdown) due in part to the inadequacy of their conceptual implements. Society at large cannot be fully explained, nor its future predicted, by universal laws of analytical methods derived from natural science. As conventional economics cannot be relied upon to provide accurate accounts of social and economic realities, nothing short of a new epistemology and not a new paradigm is required.

The disconnect between the soft and hard sciences needs to be bridged to formulate the new epistemology that would be both integrative and transdisciplinary. As capitalism has been demonstrated to have severe shortcomings, a different mode of socioeconomic organization is needed. Nabudere terms this new mode "agricology," a form of agricultural production that he deems to be holistic and integrative. Agricology is linked to Afrikology, the latter being the guiding philosophy to overcome the dichotomies, contradictions, and disconnect between mind and body caused by the perceived irrelevance of Cartesianism and Western thought generally to African issues.

Nabudere continues his criticism of Western epistemology, which in his view, created an irreconcilable divide between mind and matter. He believes that this divide is also responsible for the innumerable crises of modern knowledge and existence. Just as Diop advocated the primacy of ancient Egyptian knowledge systems, Nabudere suggests that there is an urgent need for recuperation of those systems, which are also claimed as part of black civilization. Such a program of recovery would redress the incompleteness, contradictions, and disconnects caused by Cartesian rationality. This is the key thesis of Afrikology.

The project of recuperation of black history is characterized by different trends. Some scholars outside the accepted channels and disciplines of academia take it upon themselves to disprove the idea of black inferiority by identifying significant milestones in black history and culture. They employ textual material drawn from authors such as Herodotus and Diodorus as well as biblical sources. Another trend in black historical retrieval, which counts personages such as Booker T. Washington, Chancellor Williams, and W. E. B. Dubois, believes that blacks had a visible hand in building ancient Egyptian civilization. The third school, to which, Diop, Theophile Obenga, Yosef Ben-Jochannan, and Williams belong, harnesses their considerable multidisciplinary skills in constructing a representative historiography that opposes the presuppositions of colonialist historiography.

At this juncture, Nabudere discusses the work of Martin Bernal, whom he considers to be of the integrationist school. According to him, Bernal importance lies in stating that the origins of human knowledge are to be found in ancient Egypt. He also questioned the methodologies of traditional scholars of proto-history who ignored the efforts of scholars who did not belong to their stripe.

A fourth tendency, black historiography is opposed to Eurocentric diffusionist theses and has scholars such as Diop, Obenga, and Joseph Ki-Zerbo as its pioneers.

The mentioned scholars question Western culture-centric conceptions of Africa by enlisting a startling spectrum of multdisciplinarity involving "the natural sciences, the humanities and core social science disciplines of anthropology, political science, history, Egyptology, history of art, literature, linguistics and philosophy" (Nabudere 2012: 119). The Eurocentric construction of Africa was particularly taken up by the discipline of anthropology, which depicts the racialized Other as its sole preserve. The Other fixed within a delineated spacio-temperal order marked by anthropology is a speechless object. Anthropologist Johannes Fabian pointed out that anthropology is invariably delimited in its constructs of the Other by factors of history, temporality, and ideology, which would ultimately place the anthropological project in parenthesis (1983). Anthropology had been created as a special enclave for the mute, colonized Other. The Other within this preconceived enclave was denied the capacity for speech and thought apart from the fragmented mutterings sanctioned by the anthropological project. Anthropology also provided the Enlightenment an intellectual as well as an ideological basis on which to embark on the plunder and exploitation of subject peoples and cultures.

In identifying the temporality of anthropology, some African scholars have been able to resist its pervasive power. This resistance has come in the form alternative versions of the African subject in history such as that offered by Valentin-Yves Mudimbe in *The Invention of Africa: Gnosis, Philosophy, and the Other of Knowledge* (1988). In the wake of decolonization, African anthropologists such as Archie Mafeje, Kwesi Prah, and Ben Magubane question the assumptions and motives of anthropology regarding the African subject.

The denigration of the racialized Other was eventually linked to biblical sources via what Nabudere calls "a strange migration of meaning" (2012: 125). The Hamitic hypothesis claims that peoples of black descent are afflicted with the "Hamitic Curse," through which they are destined to be "the servant of servants" (ibid.) Nabudere reminds us that race as a marker was not alluded to in the original biblical account and thus, "the strange migration of meaning" (ibid.) in which race becomes paramount. In previous times, the Curse of Ham provided the Jews with the justification to oppress the Caananites. Later, the same curse served as the basis for Arab and European exploitation of blacks. It was from this ideological context that the Hamitic Hypotheis, which states that anything of value that exists in Africa was brought there by the Hamites, became possible. The hypothesis not only entailed the non-African exploitation of blacks, but also legitimated the willful fracture and erasure of African culture and history. In addition, the hypothesis culminated in "scientific racism," which manifested itself in the extermination of natives in the New World and black enslavement in Old World.

A discursive countermeasure to racial denigration developed in historical studies undertaken by Africans themselves. In inscribing the African presence in historical discourse, blackness within the ancient kingdoms of Egypt, Nubia, and Ethiopia was invoked. Orality came to be seen as key feature in the constitution of African historical material. Jan Vansina is noted to have been at the vanguard of this mode of historiography (1985). Vansina was often not regarded as a proper historian but as an ethnologist or an ethno-historian. This perception is one which even African historians had to confront. They had to prove the conceptual validity of their intellectual endeavors while at the same time attempting to recuperate the value of the past in history within a present that dictated urgent anti-historical concerns.

A school of subaltern historiography emerged from Dar es Salaam under the intellectual leadership of Isaria N. Kimambo and Arnold J. Temu (1969). Their approach seeks to develop a historical approach that made sense to Tanzanians and, by extension, Africans beyond the strictures of Eurocentric models. Needless to add, the work of Temu and Kimambo was questioned within Eurocentric circles and academia. However, it found formidable support in Walter Rodney (1974), whose own work promoted a strong Afrocentric viewpoint. Along with Vansina, Jacob Egharevba's account of the ancient Benin kingdom also adopted orality as a key methodological feature (Usuanlele and Falola 1994). Philip D. Curtin (1981), argues for a historiography that was basically interdisciplinary in nature and which combined "the histories of agriculture, urbanisation, and social and economic relations" (cited in Nabudere 2012: 133). Curtin also questions the privileging of writing over speech. In this sense, speech encapsulates both recuperable history and tradition, through which culture becomes legible and invaluable. The point, in this case, would be to emphasize the multi-dimensionality of social existence.

Nabudere finds fault in Curtin's advocacy of interdisciplinarity, since its basis as separate academic specialties is riddled with prejudice and racism inherent in the imperial paradigm from which it emerged. Academic disciplines, individually or collectively, under the rubric of interdisciplinarity, require a radical transformation of their aims and objectives in order to reflect an authentic Africanity and its multivalent sociality. However, Nabudere appears to agree with Curtin's argument that an interiority must constitute the essence of African history rather than an exteriority driven by non-Africans bent on enforcing a cultural binarity that pronounces their innate superiority.

African historians, empowered by decolonization, opposed Eurocentric historiography in relation to Africa, which characterized the continent as "before" and "after" the advent of colonization and modernity. The perception of Africa before the intrusion of the colonial process was one mired in stasis and distinctive by its emptiness and nothingness, while the notion of after was deemed to be marked by progress, dynamism, and change. The epistemologies that undergird academic disciplines do not address an entrenched history of structural racism. In fact, they were assembled in a large part by that history, which they do much to reinforce. In order to subvert that history, they themselves would need to be reconstituted. The practical consequences of challenging the assumed universality of the traditional academic disciplines would be for Africans to rediscover their histories and lost cultures using sources of orality, in which griots and experts of orature (a term coined by Ugandan scholar Pio Zirimu in an attempt to avoid an oxymoron, the term means literature delivered by word of mouth) would play a prominent role.

Comparative linguistics became a vital area of study in linking ancient Egypt with black Africa. Diop and Obenga argued during the UNESCO symposium held in Cairo, in 1974 "The Peopling of Ancient Egypt and the Deciphering of Meroitic Script", that the ancient Egyptian language belonged to the linguistic tree of black Africa. In particular, Diop argued that ancient Egyptian civilization was essentially Negroid in form and content. This thesis forms the kernel of his *The African Origin of Civilization*, in which he employs his knowledge of the natural sciences to advance his arguments.

Nabudere agrees with Curtin that the existing corpus of academic disciplines is not able to produce representative knowledge concerning Africa. Interdisciplinary and transdisciplinary approaches need to be developed to address the multifarious nature of African existential realities. The inauguration of transdisciplinarity as a paradigm for academic study would redirect not only the course of African historiography but also the trajectory of world history as a whole.

Similarly, the geographical entities carved out by colonialism are a caricature of true African territorial dynamics. Vindicationalism, a school of pan-Africanist thought that espouses strong beliefs proclaiming an African renaissance and emancipation, can be viewed as yet another effort to inscribe the African presence on a canvas marred by multiple forms of colonial violence and erasure. The African resistance to Western culture-centric discourses on the African continent led to the discrediting of functionalist anthropology which had demonstrated itself to be a handmaiden of the colonial project.

Diop points out that Pythagoras spent twenty-two years learning Heliopolitan cosmology from Egyptian priests; Plato and Eudoxus spent thirteen years on the same endeavor; and Democritus spent five years. According to Diop, ancient Egypt and not Greece was the foremost site of global culture and learning. Diop's efforts to prove the African origins of ancient Egypt place a serious question mark on the validity of colonialist African history.

Diop claims that Plato plagiarized Egyptian sources in *Timaeus* and that Greek scholars are often guilty of misinterpreting those same texts. Traditionally, Eurocentric scholarship emphasized the non-existence of African history and, by extension, philosophy. Nabudere agrees with Diop, by stressing the impressive cultural achievements of ancient Egypt. Nabudere, not unexpectedly, rails against the Western characterization of African systems of thought as exotica and irrational exempla.

Western discourses on Africa in the social sciences, including anthropology, tend to reflect the prevailing intellectual fashions of specific epochs such as evolutionism, diffusionism, functionalism, structuralism, and poststructuralism (Nabudere 2012, 154). Nabudere has reservations about the failure of Mudimbe and Kwame Anthony Appiah to adequately demonstrate the validity of indigenous African systems of thought about which they seem to be uncomfortably apologetic. He argues that Mudimbe and Appiah are concerned with questions arising out of the possible exteriority of African philosophy motivated by Western anxieties. He also adds that the manner in which the authors attempt to frame the foundational problematic in African philosophy is indelibly indebted to a Western paradigm, which in any case, at best, ignores African cultures, and at worst, denigrates them. In the quest to retrieve a lost or fractured philosophical heritage, Nabudere indicates that the work of Diop and Obenga is the way forward.

Nabudere also questions Paulin Hountondji's notion of "extraversion," which is concerned with the expatriation of African intellectual manpower and knowledge forms to the West. In Nabudere's view, this particular situation can be combated by political awareness and mobilization. In other words, African forms of agency are what is required. In more telling terms, the academic specialty of African Studies, Nabudere argues, is fundamentally enmeshed in a foreign-designed framework that occludes what ought to be legitimately African concerns and objectives. In order to produce ideologically relevant philosophies, the entire paradigm, in which knowledge is developed and disseminated, would have to be transformed.

Functionalist anthropology is implicated in a flawed epistemology that separates knowing subject from known object, even as the latter ought to be a participant. The truncated knowledge produced within the context of this epistemic equation leads, according to Nabudere, to an even more problematic issue, which is the irreconcilable gulf between mind and body. This division has given rise to the divided self, which is rendered invariably incomplete. In addition, through this separation, the false and unending problematic between the Same and Other was inaugurated.

The mathematicization of everyday life initiated in the era of Galileo was, in Nabudere's view, another category mistake, i.e., in substituting natural languages when not appropriate with the language of mathematics. Functionalist anthropology, just as other disciplines within social science, adopted the methodologies of the natural sciences together with inappropriate epistemologies in producing knowledge that was flawed at its foundations. This is an error that has resulted in most of the problems of contemporary society.

In his bid to realize the aims of Afrikology, Nabudere contends that orality should be at the center of African epistemic projects. A general African worldview states that speech and tradition are the primary sources of all knowledge. For example, traditional Bambara society has terms for custodians of knowledge (doma) and wisdom (soma), signifying knowledgeable individuals. In this sense, knowledge has a sentient quality in that it is connected rhythms of everyday life.

Nabudere claims that the necessity for abstract thought within the African context becomes redundant. Without alluding to it, Nabudere's thought converges with négritudist beliefs. In fact, much of his thought can be construed as a resurrection of négritude (the literary and philosophical position, developed by francophone African intellectuals in France during the 1930s, that held that the best strategy to oppose French colonialism was to encourage a common racial identity for black Africans worldwide) under another name in the manner its establishes and reinforces a supposed dichotomy between black and Caucasian thought.

The Cartesian dichotomy between mind and body ought to be bridged in order to effect a "reconvergence." In the Galileo-Cartesian, and in fact, North Atlantic tradition as a whole, the compartmentalization of knowledge forms and areas into independent entities is what is responsible for the fragmentation of perception regarding social reality. Nabudere would ultimately argue that the rejection of metaphysics, which is a prominent legacy of the Western Enlightenment, is also the cause of social and epistemic fragmentation.

African systems of knowledge were vilified and repressed by the colonial authorities because they were considered potential sources of subversion. Colonialism, as we would recall, was not merely a seizure of African territories; it was also a willful replacement of African worldviews with Eurocentric ones. In other words, it entailed the entire transformation of consciousness. So colonialism accomplished its aims along three main sites; the supposed virgin expanses of land, the body of the colonized, and the mind of the subject. As a result of the suppression of African knowledge forms, they were forced underground and thus thrived within secret societies and other clandestine circles. Nabudere avers that Gadamer recognizes the importance of orality and communication as fundamental requirements of knowledge preservation and transmission. They both form part of his notion of hermeneutics which is concerned with the reconstitution of knowledge in the light of the strictures and excesses of modern science.

Afrikology, as Nabudere constantly argues, is the philosophy by which humankind can overcome the multiple problems of contemporary society. Within the African context, a significant part of these problems is evident in the contestation between the wealthy urban dwelling elite and the impoverished rural dwellers, whose systems of knowledge and way of life are structurally devalued. Within such a context, the dimensions of conflict assume economic, social, epistemic, and cultural manifestations. This lack of social cohesion, according to Nabudere, is what has led to the stagnation of African cultures and societies.

Language, the basis by which speech and communication are possible, is a vehicle that can serve to heal and strengthen society. Language is also a veritable repository of knowledge as Julius Nyerere, for example, sought to demonstrate by translating William Shakespeare's Julius Caesar into Kiswahili. Ngugi wa Thiongo attempted to do the same by writing in Gikuyu.

Nabudere stresses that the issue of language is of vital significance because no academic discipline is capable of capturing the multifarious dimensions of African knowledge or the scope of wisdom and information contained in African languages. Nabudere, in a rather sudden manner, proceeds to extol the virtues of pan-Africanism as a restorative philosophy and program of political action. He also advances the cause of indigenous knowledge systems (IKS), which he admits would have to contend with the centuries-long dominance of science. IKS and science need to exist within the same space even when they would tend to be in opposition to each other. Once again, Afrikology – in this instance, termed a "universal epistemology" – is posited as the framework through which the contradiction can be managed.

Finally, Nabudere rejects transhumanism, which purports to improve the human species through the development of science and technology. Instead, he argues for the umpteenth time for the benefits of Afrikology, while drawing parallels with ancient Egyptian cosmology.

4

The Universe and Philosophy
Before Socrates

Dani Nabudere's later focus on the concept of Afrikology, apart from having unambiguous ideological implications, broaches on areas of knowledge that demand considerable expertise. If his claim that Africa is the Cradle of Humankind is not to be reduced to a mere rallying cry, it must be interrogated for its scientific credentials. Nabudere's posture is one that announces his postulations need to be taken seriously. The nucleus and beginnings of the concept of Afrikology can be located in protohistory as the academic specialty that provides the grounds for its scrutiny and ultimate legitimation.

Wim M. J. van Binsbergen's work, *Before the Presocratic* (2012) presents a kaleidoscopic assessment of regional and global epistemic traditions and configurations before the advent of ancient Greek thought (see also 2011a–d; 2012b–f; 2013). In this way, he addresses the worlds that Nabudere is so much concerned about employing: an impressive assemblage of specialties namely, protohistory, archeology, comparative ethnography, comparative mythology, comparative linguistics and genetics. His central thesis is that rather than viewing different regional epistemic formations as singular and distinct, it is more appropriate to understand them as being part of a global and historical continuum of knowledge traditions that is perpetually subject to migration and transformation – in short, all the elements of transplantation and dispersal. In this light, the strict separation between regional and ethnic knowledge becomes misguided and often preposterous.

Convincing as Van Binsbergen's arguments are, the messy phenomenon of race can undermine their appeal within the contexts and scripts of subalternity. Racial violence is not merely the abuse and denigration of subject peoples. It is means more importantly, the total annihilation, or at least, transformation of consciousness, which of course touches on questions of the intellect. Racially abused peoples are never taken seriously intellectually. This is an angle completely absent from Van Binsbergen's work as much as he attempts to advance a supposedly Afrocentric perspective.

Van Binsbergen calls into question the widespread perception held by many important philosophers – such as Heidegger and Gadamer – that the Presocratic thinkers started what is considered Western philosophy and that Empedocles initiated "the system of four elements as immutable and irreducible parallel components of reality – and in doing so, ... laid the found for Modern science and technology, and the Modern World System at Large" (ibid., 31). Afrocentrists attempt to establish the primacy of the African continent and African cosmologies, often in direct opposition to outright racist objection. Van Binsbergen's project seeks to overcome this age-long "paradigm of oppositionality" for a broader outlook of interconnectedness between human knowledge and epistemic traditions. Thus globalization:

> as well as the rise of a vocal counter-hegemonic trend in scholarship all over the world, have ushered a new era, where the transcontinental continuities of the present invite us to investigate transcontinental continuities of the past, and to overcome such divisiveness as hegemonic interests of earlier decades and centuries have imposed on our image of the world and of the cultural history of humankind, and to help free Africa from the isolated and peripheral position that has been attributed to that continent in present-day World System. (ibid., 32)

Van Binsbergen also reminds us that he has conducted "counter-hegemonic, transcontinental research for over twenty years now" (ibid.). This places his Afrocentric credentials to the fore even while interrogating the radicality of those same credentials, merely because he has taken up a project whose theoretical composition includes a far-reaching incorporation of genetic science, archeology, linguistics, comparative mythology, comparative ethnography, and empiricism, in short, a range of radical methodologies that could end up signaling a whole new academic genre.

On the Pelasgian Hypothesis

According to accepted paleoanthropology, archaic Homo sapiens evolved to anatomically modern human beings in sub-Saharan Africa as early as 200,000 years ago, and then dispersed to other continents. This view is termed the "Out-of-Africa" (OOA) hypothesis (or "recent single-origin hypothesis" (RSOH), "replacement hypothesis," or "recent African origin model" (RAO) by experts in the field). There is also the "Back-to-Africa" hypothesis, according to which human beings developed elsewhere, and then returned to Africa bearing new genes, religious and cultural practices, and new knowledge pertaining to science and technology. Van Binsbergen terms this migration back into Africa "Pandora's Box." He mentions some central hypotheses that he returns to frequently in his work, notably, the Borean hypothesis, as formulated by and Harold C. Fleming (1987; 1991) and Sergei Starostin (1989; 1991), which, as described by Van Binsbergen, holds:

all languages spoken today retain, in their constructed language forms, substantial traces of a hypothetical, reconstructed language arbitrarily termed "Borean" and supposed to have been spoken in Central Asia, perhaps near Lake Baikal, in the Upper Paeleolithic (c. 25 ka BP). (2012: 34)

On the other hand says Van Binsbergen, Stephen Oppenheimer (2001) argues, using the Sunda hypothesis, which postulates:

considerable demic effusion of cultural traits took place from South East Asia to Western Eurasia (and by implication to Africa) as the South Asian subcontinent was flooded (resulting in its present-day, insular nature) with the melting of polar ice at the onset of the Holocene (10 ka BP). (ibid.)

Van Binsbergen adds that to understand prehistorical and protohistorical philosophical thought, it is necessary to move beyond the philosophical enterprise as conceived as a narrow academic discipline and instead take in the study of the language, culture, and the social context in which Presocratic thought evolved. Accordingly, this methodological imperative necessitates a multiplicity of disciplinary competencies. In relation to philosophy itself, he states that he does not offer a clear-cut argument per se, but instead presents a "historical and transcontinental-comparative *prolegomena* to an ontological philosophical argument on cosmology and the structure of reality" (ibid., 41). Van Binsbergen labels his approach as "counter-paradigmatic" inasmuch as it seeks to "chart intellectual *terra incognita*" (43).

While the conventional discipline of Global Studies deals with specific cultures, Van Binsbergen's course is very much concerned with entire continents and the concept of globality itself. Thus, he begins from the Upper Palaelithic Age as a spatial construct while at the same time tracing "a particular intellectual cultural complex characterized by such features as cyclicity, transformation and element cosmology" (ibid.), thereby bypassing "the highly presentist and localist perspectives prevailing in social anthropology ever since the *classic*, fieldwork-centered tradition in that field was established in the 1930s–1940s" (ibid.). In addition, he learned that, within a given social context, cultural meaning is not only produced by social, political, and economic factors alone – he considers this a largely reductionist perspective – but also by symbols capable of retaining meaning and relevance across several cultural and geographical divides.

Karl Jaspers had propounded the notion of Achsenzeit (Axial Age: the period from 800 to 200 BCE, during which, according to Jaspers, similar new ways of thinking appeared in Persia, India, the Sinosphere and the Western world; see Jaspers 2011), which, barring its overt Eurocentric connotations, as Van Binsbergen reminds us, is central for an understanding of the concept of transcendence that became entrenched in human thought after the convergence of writing, the state, organized religion, and the monetary economy as key factors in the organization of society. Due to different waves of proto-globalization, these crucial features of organized society found their way into different regions of the globe such as the Aegean by way of Iran and China via Northern India. Those transformative busts of proto-globalization were powered by chariot, horse-back, and water transport.

Van Binsbergen argues that certain cultural traits from the Upper Palaelithic Age found their way into the African continent and he first became aware of this when conducting fieldwork in Francistown, Botswana where geomancy, a supposedly indigenous divination system, displayed strong similarities with "an Islamic astrologically-based divination system that was established in Iraq around 1000 CE that in the meantime spread not only to Southern Africa but also to the entire Indian Ocean region, West Africa, and even Medieval and Renaissance Europe" (2012: 44). Geomancy, and other similar diagnostic and therapeutic traditions all have a formal character that facilitates their transmission across several spacio-temporal contexts. Similarly, it is possible to study the correlations between cultural features – such as animal symbolism (such as the leopard and its spotted pelt) myths, and games belonging to the mancala (a board-game) variety – from a largely transcontinental perspective (see Van Binsbergen 1995).

Transcontinental Studies, Van Binsbergen points out, has led to significant shifts in anthropological research and the global politics of knowledge, fostering in the process the rise of disciplines such as postcolonial theory, Afrocentrism, Mediterranean Bronze Age Studies, and Egyptology. In this regard, the work of American sinologist, Martin Bernal is central – especially the thesis elucidated in his *Black Athena* (1987–2006).

Van Binbergen then defines "strong Afrocentrism as a theory that considers Africa the origin of crucial phenomena of cultural history" (2012: 46). This aspect immediately connects with Nabudere's notion of Afrikology, which essentially regards Africa as "the Cradle of Humankind," and Afrocentric theorists such as Molefi Kete Asante, whose notion of Afrocentrism possesses quite a number of arresting subtleties quite distinct from the usual ethnocentric affirmation of Africa's cultural primacy. Van Binsbergen is always anxious to affirm his Afrocentricity; one of the ways in which he accomplishes this is by attempting to debunk "the Eurocentric and hegemonic myth that philosophy started in Europe in historical times" (47).

In advancing what he terms the Pelasgian hypothesis, Van Binsbergen argues that as a result of the OOA exodus, Africans settled all over the world, bearing along with them specific sociocultural features such as marriage, kinship systems, and divination practices. In addition, during this global dispersal, myths and other products of the collective subconscious from Africa found their way into other regions of the world. Once out of Africa, these cultural manifestations became embedded in what he terms "Contexts of Intensified Transformation and Innovation," which led to "new modes of production (both within and beyond hunting and gathering), and of new linguistic macrophyla" (ibid., 49).

Contrary to the OOA hypothesis, the "Back-to-Africa" hypothesis is claimed to have occurred "in the last 15 ka" (ibid., 51), during which Asian peoples migrated to Africa carrying cultural attributes with them. These attributes pertained to kingship, ecstatic cults, divination systems, and language, as, for example, Van Binsbergen claims there are Austric similarities in Bantu. It is suggested that the return to Africa most likely happened through (1) North Africa and the Sahara and (2) along the Indian Ocean from the Arabian peninsula or a more southern point of departure through the Swahili coast, Madagascar, or via the Cape of Good Hope through the Atlantic West coast ending up in the Bight of Benin and West Africa. As a result of this migration, an Indonesian/ South East Asian influence (including East and South Asian) – otherwise termed as the Sunda influence – can be discerned at a transcontinental level which includes Africa. Van Binsbergen argues that it is possible to trace the emergence of mancala board games in Africa to an Asian origin, with world religions such as Buddhism and Islam serving as platforms for their dissemination. 'Sunda' traits such as agricultural crops, xylophones, ecstatic cults and kingship structures, it is mentioned, can also be observed in West Africa. Van Binsbergen further suggests that "Sunda-associated, Buddhist-orientated states were established in Southern and South-central Africa around the turn of the second millennium (Mapungubwe and Great Zimbabwe are cases in point)" (ibid., 64).

It is also possible to trace the history and movement of geomancy at the transcontinental level. One of the oldest textual and iconographic attestations of geomantic representational apparatus is of Chinese origin. Another ancient geomantic attestation stems from the Arabian context. It is claimed that these two geomantic systems in fact share "semantic, symbolic and representational correspondences" and hence "a common cultural environment" (ibid., 68). Apart from Sino-Tibetan and Arabian geomancy (divination by the earth) which bear remarkable similarities with each other, there is also the same family of systems to be found in ancient Greek and Latin, Hebrew, Indian and pre-modern African contexts. In Africa in particular, other systems of divination include the Malagasy *sikidy*, West African *Ifa*, and the Arabian '*ilm al-raml*. While many scholars have affirmed the influence of Arabian geomantic practices across the coast of the Indian Ocean, many Afrocentric scholars have in turn rejected the Arabian origins of the West African geomantic system. Van Binsbergen recalls the derision and resistance which met his claim that similar geomantic systems exist outside West Africa at an Afrocentric discussion group. Van Binsbergen cites Robert Dick-Read, who asserts that there is evidence of Arab/Islamic influence in West African geomancy especially Ifa, which employs the names of Islamic prophets within its corpus. So it is not inconceivable that Ifa "may have an Indian Ocean, circum Cape background" (cited in Van Binsbergen 2012: 72). Van Binsbergen concludes that West and South African practices of geomancy are directly indebted to Indian Ocean/Sunda influence coming through the Cape of Good

Hope. Also noteworthy is, in parts of Africa, there exist simple configurations of
geomancy which are likely to be derivations of more intricate forms that possess
a non-African origin most probably Chinese. This view has not been welcomed
by strong Afrocentrists. Van Binsbergen asserts that divination bowls from
Venda and West Africa are likely to be variations of Chinese divination bowls
or nautical instruments. The Sunda influence we are informed, can be discerned
in the Persian Gulf, the Mozambican-Angola corridor, the Bight of Benin, and
the Austronesian population of Madagascar. On the other hand, when Africans
surface in T'ang China, it is as slaves so much so that the figure of the black
trickster became a familiar literary trope. All of this would obviously meet with
the disapproval of Afrocentrists.

Martin Bernal who has gained the attention of Afrocentrists for mixed
reasons is viewed by Van Binsbergen to be "wrong for the wrong reasons" (ibid.,
84). Bernal is also accused of imposing his subjective views as statements of
fact and resorting to ad hominem tactics to assert his claims. In other words,
Van Binsbergen has much to fault about his work. Émile Durkheim is another
Western intellectual that Van Binsbergen exposes for shoddy work. Durkheim in
The Elementary Forms of Religious Life (1912) had made propositions regarding
Australian Aboriginals and totemism without so much as a visit to the site of
study. As such, he had theorized and hypothesized about an entire group of people
without any personally organized ethnographic evidence and without apparently
acceptable implements of comparative analysis.

Van Binsbergen stresses he is more concerned about establishing the linkages,
continuities, and connections between different continents of the world and
hence the timeliness and validity of the notion of transcontinentality. Movement,
migration and exchange, he points out, have for millennia been part of the
currency of human transactions. If such is the case, not only goods and people
have been transported far and wide but also ideas. And so it is possible to trace
the intellectual history of the world as sequences of interlinkages between diverse
systems of knowledge of which mancala and geomancy are major examples.
In addition, this absorbing history can tracked employing genetic, linguistic,
archaeological, comparative-ethnographic and comparative-mythological modes
of analysis.

Employing these given modes of analysis, it can be taken that the Presocratics
were not really the inventors of element cosmology as granted credit by the official
archives of history and philosophy but were merely clumsy and less inventive
recipients of a handed down system, primarily, in Van Binsbergen's view, from
ancient Asia and Africa. His thesis therefore seeks to affirm "the transcontinental
complementarity of the intellectual achievements of Anatomically Modern
Humans in the course of millennia" (2012: 86).

The Nkoya and Cyclicity

Van Binsbergen commences tracking of this – for the moment hypothetical – trajectory of the intellectual achievements of humanity by focusing on the Nkoya of Zambia who have been major subjects of his anthropological research. During the pre-colonial and pre-statal epochs, the Nkoya were categorized according to clans in a manner that had powerful political connotations. The clans played a key role in the use and management of natural resources, the economic life of communities, the deployment of rituals, and the performance of communal obligations. Within the context of precoloniality, leadership of the clans tended to be ritualized as opposed to being actually political and mostly consisted of women. However, with the advent of long distance trade and conflict among competing nationalities, the practice and visage of kingship were altered in which they became, for one, usually male-dominated and largely politicized as opposed to being merely ritual. Van Binsbergen hypothesizes that this development may also have been the mark of Sunda influence. Similarly, the existence within Nkoya culture of "iron working, Conus shell ornaments, and the introduction of a new type of xylophone-centred royal music" (ibid., 90) is enough to suggest the influence of some transoceanic involvement possibly stemming from South Asia. Van Binsbergen mentions that his research on Asian-African continuities gives him reason to believe that the transformation of Nkoya political institutions and aspects of their material culture most probably owes much to interactions with Bantuids from South Asia.

The Nkoya, being perceived by colonialist anthropological researchers as primitive, were susceptible to the biases of totemism studies, which tended to objectify the cultures of such so-called primitive tribes in terms of pairs, which are both oppositional and complementary. Accordingly, Nkoya clan names can be analyzed according to binaries that are both complementary and are in opposition. Van Binsbergen goes on to posit that there is "evidence of a more complex and more dynamic structure of threesomes that transcends recursive repetition" (ibid., 94). He mentions that he is not able to obtain the desired degree of certainty regarding many details about the clan names or their origins from native informants. Although he able to establish some continuities between the Nkoya and Taoist systems of binaries, he concludes that rather than maintain its structure and stability, the Nkoya system had degenerated "into aberrant multiplicity" (106). In essence:

> in the Taoist system the same five elements always play, in turn, the role of the destructor, destroyed, catalyst, but in the Nkoya system those roles have become disconnected hence the number of elements, or clans, has multiplied from six to eighteen. (ibid.)

The Nkoya system is not unique. Instances of element cosmology can be found in Chinese Taoism, Egyptian cosmology, and in other systems found in Africa, North America, India, Japan, and Ancient Greece.

The Engima of Empedocles

In ancient Greece, the four-element cosmology or the quadripartite conception of the cosmos (*materiae primae*, prime matter) – earth, water, air, and fire – was first adopted by Empedocles, shaman and philosopher of Acragas, and historically credited with founding the scheme. Van Binsbergen debunks this view, claiming that the scheme was already in existence at least two millennia before the Empedoclean formulation. He argues that until the early twentieth century, Empedocles was considered responsible for the system in most of the literature when fresh readings of Homeric and Hesiodic texts affirmed the opposite.

Following Empedocles, Plato and Aristotle also adopted the scheme, which eventually became the foundation of "Western natural science, astrology, medicine, psychology, literary and artistic symbolism and iconography including color symbolism until into Early Modern Times" (ibid., 109). The scheme can be found in esoteric practices of mystery cults, the Ancient Sabaceans of Yemen, the alchemy of the Qarmatians, Islamic occult sciences, and even digital media games within the context of postmodernity.

According to Van Binsbergen, Empedocles "merely codified and corrupted" a system that had been used all over Eurasia for several millennia. Thus, the influence of Asian shamanism on Greek rationalism, through its spread by Empedocles, has always been discernible.

Shamans are understood to be special individuals gifted with powers of healing and who are able to move along the celestial axis and within the Underground in search of medicine and information to heal needy and afflicted individuals and communities. Usually distinguished by a strange and bewildering disposition, it is believed that apart from Empedocles, other shamans (the healer-sage, *iatromantis*) within the classical Greek tradition include: Pythagoras, Parmenides, Abaris, Orpheus, Aristeas, Epimenides, and Hermotimus. The lives of these historical figures are usually marked by life-transforming journeys to retrieve lost souls, as in the case of Pythagoras, who ventured into the underworld to fetch the soul of Hermotimus, or Empedocles, who claimed to be able to control not only the weather but also had the power to rescue lost souls from Hades. Most of these figures were usually multi-talented, combining the roles of magician and naturalist, poet and philosopher, preacher, healer, and public counsel (Bruce J. MacLennan cited in Van Binsbergen 2012: 112).

Within classical Greek rationalism, there is the traditional opposition between Apollo and Dionysus, where the former is supposed to act as a "mitigating and balancing" influence on the latter's wild practices of ecstatic religion. Traces of this shamanic influence can be perceived in the ancient Near East and in Egypt a millennium before the emergence of the Presocratics. The process of the transmission of these shamanic influences into the Aegean was aided by the healers of ancient Iran and the Mesopotamian Magi in addition to the Scythians and Thracians.

Rather than the four-element model of Empedocles, the five-element system was more widely practiced in Greek and Roman antiquity, in which the fifth element is the quintessence. The five element model also exists in several parts of Eurasia, such as Japan and China, and in religions such as Hinduism (pancha mahabhuta), Buddhism (skandha), and the Bon religion of Tibet. In addition, it can be found among the Daisanites and among the followers of Baroaisan of Edessa.

The transformation cycle of these elements and their correlative systems are important to understand:

> human-existential dimensions (the heavens, minerals, animal life, plant life, kinship, politics, colours, music, topography, etc.) so that the entire cosmos can be subsumed in a matrix whose columns define symbolic domains and whose rows define cosmological/existential dimensions. (ibid., 118–119)

Correlative systems also provide invaluable information in the pursuit of divinatory arts and knowledge.

In the Chinese Taoist cycle of transformation, there is the belief that the difference between the elements is "accidental and situational," meaning that each may be transformed to the next within a couple of steps, thus making the distinction between them "ephemeral and non-essential," both of which establish the concept of immanentalism in Taoist thought.

Transcontinentality at Large

The presence of four or more element systems can be perceived in sub-Saharan Africa, with the Nkoya, in Van Binsbergen's view, being one of the most obvious examples. There is also an example to be found in the Yoruba of West Africa, whose model is complicated by the collective belief in an omnipresent sky god, Olorun, and the demiurge, Obatala. However, in spite of these two major attributes, Van Binsbergen posits, "the pantheon of Yoruba gods does have strong reminiscences of the Hesiodic and Egyptian cosmology" (ibid., 123) and its attendant transformation cycle of elements.

The Yoruban pantheon of deities necessitates a few words. Olorun, who resembles the Nyan-kupon of the Tshis, the Mawu of the Ewes, and the Nyonmo of the Gas, is the embodiment of the sky. As the counterpart of the Eygptian god, Pet, he is viewed as being too removed from the affairs of ordinary human beings, and so he is not directly consulted by them. As such, he has no priests or shrines to his name, which is only invoked when lesser gods are unable to intercede on behalf of mortals.

Obatala, who was conceived by Olorun, stands in place for Olorun in overseeing the affairs of heaven and earth. He is also believed to be a sky god with human endowments and seen to be the counterpart of the Egyptian god, Ptah. Being a judge of human beings, he is also deemed to have qualities that match another Egyptian god, Osiris. Odudua, Obatala's spouse, bears similarities with Isis, the Egyptian goddess, but being a promoter of the ethos of love, she is akin to the Egyptian god Hathor. Odudua gave birth to male child, Aganju, and a daughter, Yemaja. Aganju represents land (earth) while Yemaja is a water goddess. The children of Obatala and Odudua married, bearing a son named Orungun, who proceeds to sire the following children with his mother:

> Dada, a vegetable god (WOOD); Shango, lightening god (FIRE?); Ogun god of iron (METAL) and war; Olokun sea-god; Olosa, lagoon god; Oya, Niger god (sic): Oshun, river-god; Oba river-god; Orisha Oko, god of agriculture; Oshosi, god of hunters; Oke, god of mountains; Aje Shaluga, god of wealth; Shankpanna, small-pox god; Orun, the Sun (FIRE?); and Oshu, the [M]oon. Oshumare, the rainbow, is a servant of Shango, and his messenger Ara is the thunderclap; his slave is Biri, the darkness [CHAOS]. Shango hanged himself but did not die, for he went into the earth and there became a god (orisha) Ifa, god of divination, who causes pregnancy, and presides over births. Elegba, a phallic divinity; his symbol is a short knobbed club, which was originally intended to be a representation of the phallus. Circumcision and excision are connected to his worship. Ogun, the war-god. The priests of Ogun take out the hearts of human victims, dry and powder them, mix them with rum, and sell them to people who wish to acquire great courage (ibid., 124).

In spite this elaborate pantheon of gods, foursome features – bearing similarities to four-element cosmology or reflecting the accepted quadripartite separation of the cosmos – are noticeable in the Yoruba context in the form the "four estates, four winds, four days of the week, four walls of the Yoruba kingdom and a divine foursome Shango/Oya/Oba and Oshun" (ibid., 125). In other parts of Africa and its environs, traces of the four-element system can be found in Madagascar, which earlier scholars had attributed to an Indonesian influence, but which Van Binsbergen ascribes to a broader Sunda incursion entering Africa through South East Asia.

Apart of the four-element system, other products and practices of Sunda transmission into Africa are said to include the xylophone, the gong, and breast harp, ancient Roman coins, cowry shells, geomancy, kingship rituals, and activities of ecstatic cults. These products and practices are most likely to have traveled via the Indian Ocean through the Cape of Good Hope and then entered into Africa. Heliopolitan cosmogony is also an attestation of the four-element system, in which instances of transformation comprising destruction and regeneration are frequent.

Van Binsbergen has been an energetic contributor to the black Athena debate instigated by the work of Martin Bernal. Bernal argues that much of the ancient Greek civilization is indebted to ancient Egypt, a line of thinking promoted by Diop. Initially, Van Binsbergen departs from the two opposing authors by arguing that the ancient Greek myth of Hephaestus and Athena owes much to Central Mediterranean and Anatolian influences rather than to Egyptian inspiration. He was later compelled to reconsider his position, agreeing with Bernal in the process, after a closer reading of Ovid and Virgil in relation to the contested myth. In other words, he reached an Egyptianizing conclusion. However, this conclusion is demonstrated to be only partial, as he goes on to argue, "some rudimentary transformative cyclical element system could be a Pelasgian trait" (ibid., 140), arriving from West to Central Asia. This argument immediately debunks the conclusions of Bernal and long-established Afrocentrists such as Diop.

Van Binsbergen mentions several Pelasgian traces to be found in ancient Egypt, such as the composition of the gods, which appear to owe much to a West Asian derivation. Shamanic practices, leopard-skin symbolism, and the royal diadem, which became common in Egypt, are all, in Van Binsbergen's view, attributable to a strong West Asian influence. But it is also not in doubt that the main cornerstones of Presocratic philosophy were received from the accomplishments of ancient Egypt, which was already in decline. It is not in doubt that Empedocles's vulgar appropriation of Egyptian cosmology did much to define the climate of Greek thought, especially with regard to the espousal of the four-element doctrine.

Presocratic Greek thought was preoccupied with arriving at the meaning of ultimate reality. Different thinkers came up with different explanations, such as Thales, who identified water as the primal matter, while Anaximenes posited it was air, and Heraclitus said it was fire. Xenophanes argued that it was the earth, and Empedocles mentioned four elements, (water, air, earth, and fire). The important demarcation in Greek thought between what came before Socrates and what came after was established by Hegel and Schleiermacher, while Aristotle is credited with asserting the significance of Empedocles in a manner that was to have a profound effect on "Graeco-Roman, Arabic, Indian, and European natural science, astrology, other forms of divination, medicine, iconography" (ibid., 150), thereby creating the main epistemes of modern science and thought. A major shift occurred in the four- element system between the time it was conceived within Taoism and "the ontologies of Graeco-Roman late antiquity, medieval Byzantine, Arabic, and Latin Science and their Early Modern Derivative" (ibid.). Under the later appropriations, the system became fixed, rigid, and standardized, through which the issue of transformation no longer mattered. As such, the elements no longer mutated from one substance to another, but remained unchanged, as established under the Empedoclean system (*rhizomata*), even when interacting with other elements, which is not the case within the context of the original Taoist system.

The transition from the fluidity of the element system in its Taoist phase to its standardized form in its Empedoclean orientation coincided with the shift from an illiterate, oral mode of knowledge progressing to a written format, which, in turn, signaled the emergence of the state, science, and organized religion as major organizing factors within culture and society. It also implied the entrenchment of the notion of transcendence in place of the Taoist concept of immanentalism.

Van Binsbergen is also able to track the global distribution of flood myths from a protohistorical perspective (2008). In Judaism, the tears of Archangel Michael are believed to have created the Cherubim (a group of angels), just as in the Taino culture, Jamaica, rain is perceived to be divine tears. Both of these myths bear similarities to the Egyptian mytheme regarding "human beings from divine tears." The mytheme of divine tears producing human beings correlates to leopard symbolism, in which its spotted skin is akin to rain. Also of interest in this connection are the rites associated with the planting season, with its tropes of abundance and fertility, just as communal rites of sexual promiscuity and ancient observances in memory of the dead.

To return to the Empedoclean corpus: It was believed that the four elements that constituted the system completed a transformation cycle and this rendering was adopted by both Plato and Aristotle. Those who came after them, on the other hand, believed that the four elements consisted of four distinct, separate, immutable ontological substances, which, accordingly, privileged the concept of *rhizomata* over the contrary Empedoclean understanding and articulation of *effluvia* (the elments that enter through the sense organs).

Empedocles, to be sure, reflected upon the relations between mutability and immutability and sought a resolution between the two, thereby formulating a theory of element relations, as opposed to Parmenides, who adopted a stance of uncompromising immutability. Thus, in the Empedoclean and the Aristotelian tradition of the four-element system, fire, air, water, and earth are deemed to originate from each other, with each of them bearing a direct relation to each other. This much is made clear in Aristotle's *Meteorologica*.

Binbergen reminds us that the Western intellectual tradition generally does not fully recognize the significance of the notions of transformation and cyclicity within Empedoclean cosmology, although this is gradually changing. A number of modern scholars interpret the transformative dimension of the cosmology as a perpetual transition between Love (*philia*) and Strife (*neikos*). In this instance, Love is symbolized as a spherical state embodying all the cosmic elements, which eventually disintegrates under the influence of Strife; then the cycle of spherical embodiment and tumultuous disintegration is resumed once again. This abbreviated modern interpretation of Empedoclean cosmology can, in turn, be compared with the simple movement of the pendulum, or, more appropriately, as moving in a cyclical fashion, between production and destruction on one level, and fusion (love) and separation (strife), on another.

Van Binsbergen expends a great deal of effort in discovering the origins of the quadripartite division of the cosmos as couched in the Empedoclean doctrine. As mentioned earlier, he argues that Empedocles was not the originator or author of the scheme, even though Aristotle had claimed so in his *Metaphysics*. Van Binsbergen conducts his research beyond the scope of Graeco-Roman antiquity to focus on the Palaeolithic Age to find answers.

It is important to note that, apart from Empedocles, the Milesian school of philosophy upheld the Empedoclean doctrine, and to note that Heraclitus, the author of the doctrine, was aware of the significance of cyclicity within it. Nonetheless, the spread and influence of foursomes in the symbolism and iconography of different peoples has been tremendous, including, for example, the four trigons of the zodiac; the four humors of Galenus (blood, black bile, yellow bile, and phlegm); the four stages of man (gold, silver, bronze, and iron); and the four virtues, namely justice, fortitude, prudence and temperance (ibid., 176). In addition, there are four cardinal truths in Buddhism, which are: the meaning of life is suffering, the source of suffering is attachment, there is a possible end to suffering, and there is a route available to the end of suffering. Other major foursome symbolisms and iconography include the four men of the Apocalypse; the four distinct suits of the deck of cards notably clubs, diamonds, hearts and spades; the four categories of Arabian music theory; the four main characters of Chinese opera; the four major castes of India; the books of the Veda with each consisting of four parts; the interlinked parts of the Kabbala; the four Archangels; and the four lights of Gnostic mysticism.

Van Binsbergen concludes that many of these foursomes are based on the four-element system, while some others not mentioned here, are not. He also mentions a couple of instances in the field of pure science devoid of human agency where foursomes play major roles, such as in physics, where there is a quest to arrive at a unifying theory through the combination of gravity, electromagnetic force, strong nuclear force, and weak nuclear force. There is also the four-color problem in mathematics, and the reality that each DNA and RNA protein comprises a blend of four different amino acids among other noted examples.

Van Binsbergen's major academic aim is to find evidence of the four-element system existing before Graeco-Roman antiquity. Therefore, he begins his search in the African Palaeolithic Age, which offers scant and perhaps unreliable information apart from the Blombos Cave red ochre block in South Africa and rock art in Zimbabwe. In carrying out this aspect of the work, he has only comparative linguistics, archaeology, comparative mythology, and comparative ethnography as disciplines upon which to rely. His quest leads to the recognition that the major

Neolithic or Bronze Age Triadic Revolution, which culminated in writing, the state, organized religion, and (proto)science becoming the major factors determining the course of human thought, culture, and civilization was indeed a revolution in more than one sense. Accordingly, this triadic revolution established the Hegelian conception of dialectics as a major paradigm, which is regarded as an advancement on binary systems comprising for instance, in the cosmological sense, heaven and earth, or land and sea. A third agent is required to overcome the endless recursion inherent in the binary model that the triadic revolution transcended and which, in turn, transformed history, society, and culture.

However, Van Binsbergen suggests that North American and African formal systems – with the notable exception of Egyptian Hermopolitan cosmology – continued to be characterized by twosomes and foursomes, and hence their delay in effecting the transition to the triadic paradigm and its attendant benefits. He adds that the Empedoclean four-element system was less advanced than the Taoist doctrine of transformation cycle, which incorporates a catalyst that endows it with a triadic structure. It is implied that African divination systems, specifically Hakata, Ifa, and Sikidy belong to "an Upper Palaeolithic Old World standard pattern" (ibid., 209). Van Binsbergen ultimately concludes that the element system could have emerged from anywhere.

Van Binsbergen then examines the work and impact of Albert Terrien de Lacouperie, the French-British Sinologist who had posited a Western origin for the inhabitants of China, thereby concluding that Europe and much of Asia shared a common ancestry in terms of civilization. Terrien produced an astonishing body of work that encompassed "contributions to the history of Buddhism and of South Asian, Central Asian and East Asian writing systems and scriptures, the ethnography and linguistic description of Formosa, the archaeology of Korea, explorations in Assyriology, and the first recognition of the striking similarities between the Indus valley and Easter Island (pseudo-)scripts" (ibid., 218). In addition, Terrien is regarded as being responsible for the emergence of pan-Babylonianism, the theory that all of civilization emanated from ancient Mesopotamia. The attention given to the Terrien's Sinology was accomplished by renewed focus on *Yi Jing (Book of Changes)*, a Chinese classical text that propounds a cosmology covering all facets of human society and the universe. Within the context of this divination system (cleromancy) that serves as an all decisive oracle, a random generator – most notably a coin – is expected to accomplish a specific result drawn from one of sixty- four possible combinations, each of which bears specific divinatory significations concerning existence and beyond.

Terrien continues to elicit considerable interest in China and Japan long after in his untimely passing. His detractors are equally many, with a noted Afrocentrist, Runoko Rashidi claiming, in contrast to Terrien's conclusions, that black Akkado-Sumerians of Elam-Babylonia were responsible for the the *Yi Jing*. Cleromancy, the divination system embodied in the *Yi Jing*, has been a source of considerable academic controversy. The text of the *Yi Jing* has been touted by local Chinese advocates to contain the kernel of all the major scientific breakthroughs, but this has been contested by many Western scholars. Advocates of the text affirm that those who approach it with patience and diligence would be rewarded with knowledge hidden within its labyrinthine and obscurantist meanings. Meanwhile, others have concluded that it is a product of an obscure Central Asian dialect, the origins and status of which can longer be traced.

Van Binsbergen's major aim is to attempt to trace continuities between different continents, regions, historical epochs with underlying, if not largely intended, implications for race. His findings lead him to conclude that Asia and sub- Saharan Africa were "part of a *multi-centred* and *multi-directional* prehistoric and protohistoric system of exchanges in which an emerging global maritime network played an increasing role" (ibid., 225), thereby attesting to a process of proto- globalization in the Bronze Age.

Through modern archaeological and epigraphical developments, it is now possible to affirm the historical validity of Chinese ruling dynasties dating back to the period of their early counterparts in ancient Mesopotamia and ancient Egypt, prompting Chinese scholars to ascribe an endogenous trajectory of development for their civilization rather than the formerly held thesis that they shared a common civilizational pool with Western Europe, which was located in ancient Mesopotamia. This development goes against Terrien's proposition, part of which ascribes a Mesopotamian origin to *Yi Jing*. Van Binsbergen points out that the old thesis espouses a non-ethnocentric and therefore anti-hegemonic slant, while the latest Chinese proclivity to privilege an endogenous path of development for its civilization betrays the same chauvinism as the old thesis had sought to avoid.

In a lengthy passage that reveals his long and often complicated relationship with Afrocentricity, Van Binsbergen states:

> Since the 1990s I have repeatedly championed the cause of Afrocentricity. This was not in order to curry favour with my African friends and colleagues (although it did in fact endear me with them). Now was it an attempt at Political Correctness, verbally compensating Africans as recognized and self-acclaimed victims of recent global history, by offering them the mere illusion of a glorious past. My defence of Afrocentricity also had to do with my awareness that once peripheral, subjugated or excluded groups – with whom I, admittedly, do identify, by birth, choice, and adoption – *may* have preserved, in their specific worldviews, knowledge of historical facts and relationships which otherwise have been expelled from collective consciousness by the hegemonic paradigms of dominant groups in the World System. (ibid., 229)

Part of Van Binsbergen's support for Afrocentricity has resulted in his attempt to discover certain "dissimulated facts" that may have been preserved in certain group memories, but which have been ignored by the dominant global knowledge paradigms, of which his Pelasgian hypothesis is an example. The hypothesis advances the claim that during the Neolithic and Bronze Age, a markedly pigmented ethnic group possessing knowledge of proto-geomancy, early metallurgy, a fire cult, a solar cult, and formative element cosmology existed in Western Asia (ibid.), which, in a way, supports a part of Rashidi's Afrocentric thesis that has been criticized for its scanty scholarship and lack of academic rigor, an accusation that has been made much of by opponents of Afrocentric discourse. Van Binsbergen suggests that during the OOA exodus, in which indigenes of the continent dispersed to other parts of the globe during the Middle Palaeolithic Age, highly pigmented people may have settled in Asia. This pigmented cluster is credited with knowledge of rudimentary metallurgy and proto-geomancy and the dispersal of these practices Westward. This heterogeneous mix of peoples is what gives rise to the Pelasgian hypothesis.

Van Binsbergen then advances another interesting proposition. The Mediterranean was populated with a broad genetic and linguistic assemblage of peoples during which the "older layers of ethno-linguistic specificities" associated with highly pigmented people were thrust to the bottom of the social ladder while the more recent layers comprising of Indo-European and Afro-asiatic speakers formed a dominant aristocratic stratum. Given this distinct social composition, the marginalized highly pigmented substratum was eventually shoved to the margins of the Old World constituted by sub-Saharan Africa, southernmost South Asia, and Australia/New Guinea, thereby giving rise to "an inveterate, old and widespread racialism" that has subsequently denounced and denied transcontinental connections between Africa, Asia and Eurasia. This is quite an interesting hypothesis, one which Van Binsbergen admits requires further exploration.

Adolf Leo Oppenheim (1966), an influential Assyriologist whom Van Binsbergen obviously respects, makes an arresting point concerning the Mesopotamian origins of divination systems. Divination later became a prominent practice in Asia and other less significant contexts, notably Japan and Etruria. The technology of writing, in places such as Mesopotamia and China, facilitated the preservation of the methods of divination and their modes of interpretation. Oppenheim makes a claim that is bound to disconcert Afrocentrists, which is that ancient Egypt does not feature in the history of the arts of divination until its final dynasties. He then throws out a challenge to succeeding generations of scholars to attempt a reconstruction of Asian intellectual history, taking in the centrality of Mesopotamian accomplishments in science and astrology, the geomantic traditions of China, and the intricate horoscope of recent India among other major intellectual preoccupations. By extension, at the transcontinental level, it would be of considerable interest to interrogate the linkages of divinatory arts between ancient Greece, ancient Sumer, ancient China, and ancient Egypt, while also exploring the similarities in comparative mythological iconography, which constitute the central conceptual intent of Van Binsbergen's project.

Van Binsbergen corroborates the widely held view that the Anatolian/Black Sea region is noted for numerous innovative developments in the history of civilization, namely the cultivation of food crops and the domestication of animals, the development of elaborate linguistic patterns, and the dispersal of the Flood myths. Accordingly, during the Neolithic period, the region was responsible for the emergence of a numerical, classificatory, and divination practice incorporating "a protoform of the transformative element cycle," which became distinctive in its structure, form, and properties. This particular crucial geomantic development was subsequently adopted in China, where it manifested itself as *Yi Jing* and the Taoist element system, and then later in Mesopotamia and Arabia, and subsequently in North Africa and sub-Saharan Africa. Afrocentrists have always claimed that geomantic divination is indigenous to Africa, but much of the evidence provided by scholarship points to the Arabian *'ilm al-raml* as the source of sub-Saharan African geomantic practices. Comparisons between sub-Saharan geomancies and other traditions, such as the Greek element system and Chinese divination practices, have been conducted and the Greek model was found to be very different from local African traditions, which were also discovered to exclude the transformative and cyclical features of the Chinese model.

Van Binsbergen draws attention to other controversial claims, such as one that holds that the *Yi Jing* most probably has a western Asian origin mediated by Hellenism and Hellenist Egypt with the Presocratics acting as agents of the transmission. On the basis of research into comparative linguistics, Van Binsbergen suggests that the invention of the transformation cycle of elements occurred in the second millennium BCE and then spread to East Asia. He is aware of accusations of Eurocentrism arising from claims such as this, but is prepared to stand by his findings all the same. This paradigmatic invention, he claims, can be perceived in the Indo-Iranian fire cult and the Lycian cult of fire and metallurgy ascribed to the deity, Hephaestus, after which the Ionian philosophers and their acolytes formalized an element system that significantly reduced its transformative and cyclical features.

At this juncture, Van Binsbergen makes a telling argument. It is possible to trace a genealogy of transcontinental continuities between different regions of the world spanning several kilometers and several years. As such, a major cultural invention with considerable paradigmatic implications at say, the extreme eastern hemisphere would eventually travel over time and space to the extreme western hemisphere, which provides a rough translation of what transcontinental continuities would mean. In relation to the global spread of element system cosmology, its prevalence seems to be attributable to its rather formalized – and therefore rigid – modes of transmission and retention. In virtually all the societies in which it was to be found, it was regarded as esoteric knowledge retained and transmitted through elaborate initiation rites organized by secret cults. This strict formalism guarded its essential character and facilitated its fluid transmission from one generation and millennium to the next and from one extreme region to the other.

The Protohistorical Legacy

The history by which the four-element system became established is quite fascinating. The Presocratics were primarily concerned with establishing what constituted primal matter, with different schools of thought selecting either earth, air, fire, or water. Within classical Greek literature, this contestation is granted dramatic form and effect, such as in the Homeric conflict between Achilles (earth) and Hephaestus (fire) against Scamander (water). Notably, Ovid's *Metamorphoses* is essentially concerned with the motif of transformation. The classical concept of transformation is, by extension, distinguished by the polarities of to kill or annihilate versus to create or to birth, or to impede versus to aid, with both polarities underlining the importance of states of flux and transformation, in which the quest for definitive cosmic stability could only prove to be elusive. Empedocles, as we know, adopted the four-element system, retaining its essential transformative character but within the context of his millennial legacy, this crucial feature is missing, although, as Van Binsbergen correctly suspects, the lingering Eurocentric presuppositions, which privilege West Asia remain.

Neolithic Mesopotamia, which is deemed to be a cradle of genetic, linguistic, and cultural diversity, is also regarded as the site of immense paradigmatic innovations. Here, in the technological field, innovations relating to metallurgy occurred, including the invention of the chariot. In the cultural sphere, the concept of transformation was established in addition to the triad and the division between Heaven and Earth. In the political realm, the state as a political entity was established. These major developments led to new levels of sociopolitical stratification, whereby racial (highly pigmented people) and linguistic (speakers of Khoisanoid and Bantu) underdogs were forced out of the dominant centers of global culture.

The concept of transformation enshrined in the element system doctrine is also associated with shamanism, which some scholars believe to have emerged as a practice in the Upper Palaeolithic Age of West and Central Asia (c. 20–15ka BP). In order to understand shamanism, Van Binsbergen enumerates two key questions; the first relates to its origins and the second concerns the possible connections between element cosmology, cyclicity, and transformation, on the one hand, and shamanism on the other. Research into the nature and possible history of leopard- skin symbolism from a global perspective provides a key starting point for this phase of the project. His view is that leopard-skin symbolism probably emerged from West to Central Asia (10–20 ka BP). The advent of shamanism is also connected with the emergence of naked-eye astronomy. Van Binsbergen lists the major symbols associated with shamanic practice notably: speckled nomenclature for leopard; speckled nomenclature for other species; ecstatic cult; therianthropy (human beings posing as animals); leopard therianthropy; leopard-skin symbolism; Exalted Insider; Sacred Outsider; Mother goddess (2012, 257).

Apart the symbols listed above, the notion of transcendence is central to shamanism because a shamanic practitioner is believed to able to enter ordinarily inaccessible spheres of reality most notably, Heaven and Earth, or the outer reaches of the galaxy and the Underworld, in search of esoteric knowledge and information usually pertaining to restoring good health in afflicted patients or at the communal level, order, and stability.

Van Binsbergen asserts that there are similarities between the Nkoya clan system and the Taoist transformation cycle – that normally includes a catalyst – which can be attributed to three possible primary factors, namely the Upper Palaeolithic Age back-to-Africa migration; Pelasgian continuities during the Bronze Age; and finally, East Asian incursions into Africa in antiquity. The first mentioned factor, which is the back-to-Africa migration, sounds convincing because the girls' puberty rites of the NaDene speaking peoples, whose languages fall under "one linguistic phylum," notably Sino-Caucasian, Sino-Tibetan, Caucasian, and Basque, are similar to Niger-Congo speaking Africans. It has also been established that there are similarities between the material cultures of Central Asia (Mongolia), North America, and Bantu-speaking Africa, especially in basketry, fishing equipment, and basic house architecture (ibid., 261). Experts working in the field of comparative mythology have been able to confirm that there are affinities in the mythological motifs of Bantu-speaking Africa and the Americas. Finally, in the field of linguistics, there are genetic connections between African macrophyla (Khoisan, Nilo-Saharan, and Niger-Congo), Eurasiatic (Indo-European), Austric, and Afroasiatic languages.

In continuing the project of tracing transcontinental associations in prehistorical modes of thought and esoteric practices, Van Binsbergen isolates some of the distinguishing features and traits associated with shamanism, such as the elongated tooth shape and particularly circle and dot incisions, which are common in most regions of the world, most notably in parts of sub-Saharan Africa, Madagascar, ancient West Asia, and the Arctic and sub-Arctic regions of North America. Circle and dot incisions are associated with tremendous personal power and are prevalent usually where leopard-skin symbolism exists. Pardivested shamans (donned with leopard skin) existed in ancient Egypt and ancient Mesopotamia but Van Binsbergen ascribes a West Asian origin to the practice of pardivestiture. This practice also became common throughout sub-Saharan Africa most notably, Southern Africa.

Similarly, Van Binsbergen points out that the Southern African divinatory foursomes bear close resemblance to indigenous American games and divinatory models. He ascribes the global transmission of these features and practices to Central Eurasia in the Upper Palaeolithic Age, a cultural transference that most probably occurred by virtue of the back to Africa migration, during which there was a significant pattern of migration from West and East Asia into Africa via the Sahara and the Indian Ocean in the last 15 ka. Apart from bearing people, this substantial migratory trend entailed a diffusion within Africa of genetic markers, technological innovations, and cultural practices. Van Binsbergen concludes that native American and sub-Saharan African divinatory and game tablets can be traced back to a much earlier origin "in Upper Palaeolithic Old World, more than 10,000 years before Empedocles" (ibid., 274).

Van Binsbergen's Pelasgian hypothesis identifies Neolithic Bronze Age West Asia as a region replete with numerous technological developments and innovative cultural traits and practices, which were subsequently disseminated to the Mediterranean, East, South, and South East Asia, Oceania, ancient Egypt, and sub-Saharan Africa, mostly among the Nkoya. Accordingly, together with the Back-to-Africa hypothesis, the Pelasgian hypothesis provides Van Binsbergen with the crucial conceptual opening to trace numerous pre-historical transcontinental continuities spanning millennia. In seeking to establish the intellectual validity of the Pelasgian hypothesis, Van Binsbergen is able to list at least eighty Pelasgian features among peoples of different races and regions who fall within the Pelasgian realm. For instance, the mythical wagtail (*Motacilla*) attests to the importance of reed in different cultures across the globe from ancient Japan and ancient Egypt to sub-Saharan ethnicities and nationalities such as the Nkoya, the Zulu, the Yoruba, and even the natives of America. In these various cultures, the reed carries powerful cosmogonic resonances that can be traced and interpreted at an interlocking transcontinental level.

Van Binsbergen reveals that his initial fascination with Afrocentricity is what led him through a trajectory in which it is now possible to track transcontinental continuities that are the main subject of his work. This fascination, in some ways, must have led to disappointment about the claims Afrocentricity makes regarding its status and its notions regarding prehistoric Africa. However, the same disappointment is mediated by startling discoveries he makes while undertaking a most interesting intellectual journey. Here, he attempts to resolve the unexpected dilemmas he has with a problematic aspect of classical Afrocentricity:

> In recent centuries, Africa and Africans have been pushed to the periphery of the World System and to the bottom of the global scale of prestige and power – resulting in their appearance as the outsiders par excellence. To counter this unfortunate and historically distortive situation, I have cherished, for decades now, the idea of Africa's continuity with other continents, even if this means that the

intra-continental cultural initiatives and achievements to be attributed to Africa appear in a more relative light of transcontinental exchanges and common origins, thus blurring what Strong Afrocentrists have claimed to be Africa's inalienable contributions to global cultural history, e.g. geomancy. Now, although, I have often expressed my sympathy for the Afrocentric perspective, the painstaking analysis of empirical data as in the present argument yet brings me to admit that Africa has always been an integral part of global cultural history at large, but hardly, since the Upper Palaeolithic (30–12 ka BP), with decisive, pan-continental impact Afrocentrists have claimed for the African continent (ibid., 278).

Of Theses and Hypotheses

Van Binsbergen's conclusions deny the essentializations of African identities, which are usually discussed as instances of extraordinary exception when they are, in fact, part of a much broader transcontinental history linking different cultures, regions, and millennia with Africa, often receiving foreign innovations in relation to knowledge and technology rather than inventing them, but all the same, being able to adapt and transform them to meet local specificities and requirements.

Van Binsbergen had wanted to advance a strictly Afrocentric position until his findings unwittingly led him against the canons of Afrocentricity, which seek to address marginality, silence, denigration, and misrepresentation. Afrocentricity is also about the establishment of relations with the texts of W. E. B. Dubois, Chancellor Williams, Cheikh Anta Diop, Théophile Obenga, Joseph Ki-Zerbo, and Molefi Kete Asante. These authors embody a specific position in which the Eurocentric marginalization of the African subject is fervently contested and undermined. This has always been a significant characteristic of Afrocentric discourse. Futhermore, Afrocentricity, in its classical orientation, claims to be the Cradle of Humankind. No advocacy of Afrocentricity in its classical or radical orientation can be complete or credible without a consistent affirmation of this stance.

If, as Van Binsbergen correctly suspects, strong Afrocentrists would have misgivings as to the Afrocentric potentials and intent of his project, most however, would applaud the courageous counter-paradigmatic turn of his approach in striking out for an area so vast and so intriguing in its possibilities as to seek to constitute an entire genre onto itself, if not a whole new discipline. This much must be admitted about his unique project.

Van Binsbergen's deflation of Afrocentricity's credibility as a discourse affirming the cultural and civilizational primacy of the black subject does not appear willful. In addition, he manages to marshal a staggering amount of evidence to corroborate most of his claims. It is now left to Afrocentrists to deploy an equally daunting academic arsenal to restore Afrocentricity's intellectual standing, thereby hoisting it up once again, as a discourse of radical critique at a safe distance from the shackles of marginality, on the one hand, and, in turn, providing a worthy discursive alternative to Van Binsbergen's astonishing series of hypotheses, on the other. For Afrocentrists to accomplish this task, a mastery of several disciplines is necessary; comparative linguistics, comparative mythology, protohistory, and genetic science, among others. Indeed, much of Afrocentricity needs to rise above mere sloganeering and establish its much-needed foundations upon an array of discourses Van Binsbergen has assembled in arriving at such unanticipated results and conclusions, which are contrary to his initial stance as an Afrocentric sympathizer and are, in fact, counter-argumentative.

This may not be exactly so, as the Afrocentric agenda is marked by different accents and aims. Afrocentricity seeks to establish the full subjectivity, creativity, and resilience of the black subject after the multiple traumas inflicted by slavery, colonization, and other forms of racial violence and subjugation, such as apartheid. It celebrates the freedom and agency of the black subject even in contexts of entrenched violence and negation. In critical terms, Afrocentricity operates beyond the simple proclamation of Africa being the Cradle of Humankind, as if this is all that is needed to soothe the injured psyche of the black subject.

Afrocentricity operates beyond the reclamation of ancient Egypt as an original site of black civilization, even though this is central to the Afrocentric agenda, as it seeks to wrest meaning, dignity, and redemption amid the fundamental violence of slavery, colonization, and racism. Afrocentricity, in the midst of these multiple forms of elemental violence, seeks to create an inimitable buttress of pathos to soothe broken communal psyches as well as embrace the future with renewed courage.

The reach and implications of Van Binsbergen's work are too immense to attempt to arrive at a definitive conclusion quickly. It deserves to be read and analyzed diligently in order to do justice to its daunting scope, scholarship, and depth. But as mentioned earlier, what is of immediate concern is its discomfort with the general and specific aspects of the Afrocentric project. Van Binsbergen hopes his work would assuage Africa's doubts regarding its participation in transcontinental passages of global knowledge production. This hope may be cold comfort for ultra-Afrocentrists, who may choose to abide with their view of Africa as the Cradle of Civilization and then proceed to point out that Africa, once again, has been relegated to the peripheries of culture in a ruthless gesture of racialized and epistemic violence.

At a deeper level, the Afrocentric agenda seeks to come to terms with centuries of racial abuse, in which slavery is its culmination and most potent expression. The process of coming to terms with the horror of this enormous injustice and then discovering the resources by which to transcend it inflects Afrocentricity with a quite specific complexion as well as trajectory, which non-victims may never fully understand in spite innumerable well-intentioned attempts. There is a chasm of mourning that must be crossed; there is a necessity to acknowledge an immense sense of loss; there exists a physical as well as collective sense of psychic dispossession with which to contend. When Afrocentricity operates at these kinds of levels, these are the conundrums it grapples with and which shapes its aims and structures its relationship with its abiding burden of loss and finally directs its continual conversation with a past that inevitably lingers and which is impossible to forget.

If approached more critically, indeed the formidable protohistorical accomplishments of Van Binsbergen's work pose serious questions to theories of blackness regarding the origins of humanity, especially if they choose to prioritize a reductionist agenda couched in a (pseudo)triumphalist proposition, in which Africa is cast as the Cradle of Civilization. This agenda would, in Van Binsbergen's morally significant terms, be the replacement of one form of racial and cultural hegemony with another. But when Afrocentricity moves beyond such narrow conceptual objectives in order to grasp the haunting as well as transformative effects of the multiple horrors inflicted on the black race, that is, when it transcends its historic traumas while at the same time managing to enlarge its creative potentialities, then it succeeds in re-formulating the conceptual singularity of its mission and its moral validity.

Indeed, Van Binsbergen intends (and largely succeeds) to establish a series of continuities across different continents, regions, races, and epochs. In other words, his project re-evaluates the conventional perceptions and assumptions regarding global history, in which unities rather than ruptures become significant. In Afrocentric terms, the project is likely to appear too general, ridding Afrocentricity of much-needed ammunition. Nonetheless, its overall academic deportment is admirable even when staunch Afrocentrists would tend to flinch from it.

The black subject in antiquity often constitutes an anomalous and marginal presence, be it in the form of the black Irish and similar instances in the Western extremity of Eurasia, or the Dallit, labeled "Untouchables" in South Asia. So the black figure, contrary to Clyde Winters's (1980) assertion that the Xia and Shang Yin dynasties were established by blacks, has repeatedly appeared as an intruder, an unwelcome presence, according to Van Binsbergen's findings and other similar archaeological and anthropological discoveries, that stands in opposition to dominant cultural, linguistic, and theoretical paradigms, thus making the "outsider" designation fit a specific racialized pattern of reception and perception.

The characteristics that define the black presence in the Bronze Age East Mediterranean include proto-Bantu-speaking features, elongated labia, round house architecture, spiked wheel trap, mancala board games, and the worship of a single supreme deity, all of which represent a counter-paradigmatic cultural and linguistic presence.

In tracing transcontinental continuities encompassing board games, geomantic practices and traditions, shamanic manifestations, linguistic revolutions, global migratory patterns, technological innovations, leopard-skin symbolism, astronomical schemas, divinatory systems, clan structures, and toponymical systems across millennia, Van Binsbergen has attempted to construct a global intellectual history of gargantuan proportions. Writing a global history of this nature cannot be a straightforward affair, especially if there are numerous earlier hypotheses to be either proved or debunked, theoretical models to be tested and cross-checked, paradigms to be re-evaluated in accordance with historical specificities, schools of thought to be re-assessed, various contestations with leading authorities in various academic fields and disciplines, attempts at resolving the intractable dilemmas of one's untested hypotheses, intellectual contradictions within one's own traditions, open anxieties about, and obvious gaps in, aspects of the project, and myriad other concerns of both personal and professional dimensions. All these problems and challenges are reflected in Van Binsbergen's work. Nonetheless, he has made a noteworthy attempt to advance a series of theses and hypotheses that deserve painstaking attention for their sheer boldness, breadth, and versatility.

5

Classical Afrocentricity

In one of Paulin Hountondji's encounters with Cheikh Anta Diop, recounted in *The Struggle for Meaning* (2002), Hountondji claims that he heckled Diop concerning proof about his hypotheses that black civilizations owe their origins to ancient Egypt. Hountondji had asked what the significance of history was if all that mattered was the future. Diop replied, saying that the Chinese could afford to be complacent about their past because no one doubted they possessed a rich ancient civilization. But Africans could not afford such luxury, subjected, as they were, to a brutal slave trade and centuries of ceaseless racial denigration. According to Diop, history must be assigned the task of restoring black Africa's dignity and humanity. In spite of Diop's ideologically loaded response, Hountondji still found Diop's theses regarding the historical continuities between ancient Egypt and contemporary black Africa unconvincing. Quite a few prominent scholars, Isidore Okpewho, for example, find Diop's theories suspect (see Asante 1987).

In this chapter, I do not focus on Diop's theories regarding the continuities between ancient Egypt and black Africa. Instead, I examine his work on black Africa itself, to ascertain its Afrocentric value and to provide a methodological contrast to Wim M. J. van Binsbergen's notion of Afrocentricity. As a pioneer of Afrocentricity, Diop's contributions are marked by specific accents that are quite different from Eurocentric notions of the concept. In my view, much of his work in this area seems convincing in debunking the long held Eurocentric idea that prior to the incursions of the white race, black Africa had no history, culture, or civilization worth talking about. This premise serves as Diop's point of departure, in support of which he presents factual data and analysis regarding the existence of black Africa's remarkable historical past.

In *Precolonial Black Africa* (1987), Diop immediately launches the task of attesting to Africa's past without so much as a preamble. First, he examines the institutional practice of slavery, particularly in what is present-day Senegal, and discovers signs of originality in the way the different castes operated. It was socially frowned upon for an individual of a higher caste to materially exploit one of a lower caste. Even if individuals were less wealthy than ones below them socially, they were expected to offer material assistance when called upon. Serfs and slaves were not social and economic outcasts, as they played important roles in the organization and maintenance of society.

Due to the relative stability of the social system, Diop posits that it did not engender revolutions against it, which would appear to be a generalization in the absence of supporting evidence. What did occur were revolts against those at the helm of the system if they were deemed to be unworthy or incompetent. In addition, this practice of slavery was not as destructive and traumatic as the Atlantic slave trade, which is estimated to have "swallowed up one hundred to three hundred million individuals, dead or shipped to America" (ibid., 142).

Diop writes, "the ennobling of a slave, even by the king, was impossible in Africa, in contrast to the customs of European courts" (ibid., 4). Again, this seems most improbable. Oshodi Landuji Tapa (c. 1800–1868) was a slave originally from the Nupe kingdom, who, by dint of his considerable intelligence and military expertise, was able to rise to the apex of the Lagos monarchial establishment during the reign of Oba Kosoko. In addition, Oshodi Tapa became a very wealthy man as a result of tributes paid to him though international trade transactions.

One of the central arguments Diop advances for the non-revolutionary disposition of slaves in Africa is that under polygamy, slaves belonging to a mother were more integrated into the family than those working under a father. Due to integration into a family, a slave was usually seen as being part of it, and hence, would have no reason to revolt. A slave belonging to a father on the other hand, was viewed as "the scapegoat for the society" (ibid.), enjoying no special privileges or allegiance from anyone. As such, the slave could be disposed of at any time without any undue grave consequences. In spite of the relative state of abjection of the slave of a father in relation to the slave of a mother, Diop writes that the existential conditions of such a slave were better than "the plebian of ancient Rome, the thete of Athens, or the sudra of India" (5). Slaves of a father's household were said to be unable to enter the full revolutionary phase because of the isolated nature of African villages. In terms of the social structure, Africa was said to possess no feudal system. These two principal conditions, that being the absence of a feudal system and the isolation of African villages, made it impossible for revolutionaries intent on overthrowing the social structure to emerge.

In Graeco-Roman society, plebs, the general body of free Roman citizens who were not patricians, were said to be responsible for radical transformations of society being that they had no real allegiance to the established order. The established order, made up of patricians, observed strict religious injunctions handed over from one generation to the other; there were priests charged with maintaining the prescribed religious observances and who could be killed if they departed from accepted codes of conduct. Under such rigid social conditions, innovation, deviance, and heresy were prohibited. The order sought only to maintain the status quo together with its beliefs and ideologies. Only plebs and foreigners could not be bothered with the values and aspirations of the established order, and it was within their midst that seeds of dissent could be found. Diop writes that state-formation processes originated in the south, ancient Egypt in particular, and this innovative political development later found its way into the transformations that led to establishment of the Greek city-states. Here, he introduces a perspective frequently advanced in Afrocentric discourse.

During the seventh century BCE, the power structure of ancient Rome comprised the king and the aristocracy, made up of the Eupatridae. The king's powers were largely symbolic and confined to the religious sphere, while the aristocracy held on to political power. In order to subvert this defined power structure, a series of kings started to side with and empower the plebs, thereby upsetting the relations of power between the royalty and aristocracy. Eventually, a system largely attributed to Lycurgus of Sparta was established, in which the powers of kings were subordinate to the senate. Diop also provides accounts regarding the emergence of tyrants as rulers, the progressive weakening of the powers of the aristocracy, and the rise of plebs as they acquired financial capital and hence political strength. The plebs were not intent on doing away entirely with aristocratic traditions. In many instances, they reproduced the very institutions of the sociopolitical class that had previously oppressed them. The plebs and aristocrats still formed alliances in marriages that were intended to store up the latter's financial fortunes. A wide range of sociopolitical contestations that transformed power relations led to the formation of Graeco-Roman democracy. It is important to note the journey toward democracy was never smooth and was, in fact, characterized by reversals, upheavals, and violence. The plebs had to fight every inch of the way to acquire and establish what they deemed to be their rights. Of course, the aristocrats responded by attempting to protect their privileges and waning powers.

At the level of ideas, Anaxagoras, Socrates, Plato, and Zeno of Citium all contributed to the broadening and consolidation of Athenian democratic traditions. Socrates in particular "contributed to freeing morals from religions, placing justice above the law, and making conscience the guide of man" (ibid., 30–31). It has been suggested that Zeno, who is considered to be the founder of the Stoic school of philosophy, propounded the idea of a universal God in conjunction with a deeper notion of democracy. However, introducing another Afrocentric perspective, Diop writes that the concept of universalism stems from ancient Egypt, which promoted the belief in the existence of a universal God whose omniscience transcends tribe, city, and nation. Christianity, which was originally a religion of the Jews, God's chosen tribe, would later adopt this creed of universalism.

Christianity's entrenchment stemmed from the persecution its earlier adherents suffered in Rome. They were became martyrs after they were thrown to wild beasts to be devoured. The canonization of the Christian faith became possible after this singular period of tribulation and sacrifice. Diop points to the influence of the cult of Isis on the evolution of Christianity as a religion. The emergent religion also borrowed many of its organizational structures from Rome in terms of the adoption of bishoprics and dioceses as key units.

Diop claims the West stagnated in the fields of culture, science, and technology until the seventh century CE, when the Arabs started to spread the latest and most advanced ideas in those fields. During the Middle Ages, Islam and Catholicism became the principal vehicles through which knowledge was disseminated and which paved the way toward modernity. In Europe, Spain attained technological preeminence due to the Arabian influence upon the prevailing paradigm in science and technology. However, the growth of both knowledge and culture was disrupted when barbarian hordes, namely Normans (Norman conquest of England in 1066) and Hungarians (during the ninth and tenth century CE), invaded Europe and reversed broad civilizational trends. Life and property became unsafe, with most monarchies being unable to guarantee peace and stability. Diop writes that this state of generalized insecurity led to the emergence of feudalism, which arose out of the widespread breakdown of law and order. Vulnerable groups flocked to lords, who were able to provide security against marauding intruders. In return for their protection, the lords demanded material rewards, which strengthened their positions politically and militarily. Within a few generations, a system of vassalage involving nobles, on the one hand, and the lower social classes (serfs) on the other, was formed. In time, the conditions of the dependent classes worsened, while the lords further entrenched themselves.

After tracing major historical developments in the West, Diop turns his attention on the central political features that were prominent in Africa "from the first to the nineteenth century" (ibid., 43). Within this period, a notable paradigmatic development was the conversion to Islam – first introduced into Africa as early as the eighth century – of the African states of Ghana, Mali, and Songhai "in the tenth century, under the influence of the Almoravide movement" (ibid.).

Diop begins with an explication of ancient Ghana's political organizational structure. However, much information is not provided about the ancient African kingdom, with Diop admitting to not having many details regarding its constitution. Ghana was eventually drained by constant attacks by the Sussu (Sosso), which was capitalized upon by Sundiata Keita, the founder of the Mali Empire, which replaced Ghana as the preeminent regional power. After the collapse of Ghana, the region was plunged into political turmoil and instability, during which procedures of succession pertaining to rulership were disrupted.

Power operates along two principal nodes: the visible and the invisible. Both realms are governed by a vitalist force, which dictates the nature and extent of an individual's power. If, for instance, a tooth or claw of a lion served as a monarch's talisman, then it was believed that to defeat the monarch, a force stronger than both the monarch and a lion had to be summoned. In battles between kings, such vitalist dimensions were said to play a crucial role in the determination of victory or defeat. The belief in this phenomenon survived the widespread incursion of Islam in sub-Saharan Africa, through which kings, instead of enlisting the services of indigenous priests and diviners, sought the assistance of marabouts and other messengers of Islam in accessing the esoteric arts. Diop writes, "metaphysics, far from constituting a minor fact in African historical sociology, was a predominant trait" (ibid., 60).

Vitalism determined the vibrancy and quality of existence, it separated life from death, in which life was all that mattered in between the natural rhythms between night and day. The forces and dynamics that established the equilibrium within this plane of ontology were respected. If and when this order was destabilized, then it was perceived as contrary to nature; a rude violation that carried severe consequences. This was the case when the rites of succession within a monarchial tradition were violated or discarded. Order had to be re-established; otherwise, "all of nature will be sterile, drought will overtake the fields, women will no longer bear children, epidemics will strike the people" (ibid., 61).

In ancient Egypt, it was believed that when the inner drive of a king decreased significantly, it meant that he was losing his life force and had to be replaced to ensure the continuity of the community and the ontological rhythms and constants associated with existence. The practice of deposing a symbolically enervated king was known in both black Africa and ancient Egypt and in the following peoples, "the Yoruba, Dagomba, Tchamba, Djukon, Igara, Songhai, Wuadai, Haussa (sic) of the Gobir, Katsena (sic), and Daoura (sic), the Shillucks, among the Mbum, in Uganda-Ruanda (sic)" (ibid., 61). Kings were associated with divinity, they were supposed to exist on a higher metaphysical plane than mere mortals. As such, "the king is truly guarantor of the ontological, and therefore the terrestrial and social, order" (ibid., 62).

Initially, Diop dwells extensively on the Songhai Empire, much more than he did on Ghana and Mali. Sonni Ali, the lukewarm Muslim and the renowned ruler of Songhai, comes up a few times for mention. But Askia Mohammad (aka Askia), former lieutenant of Sonni Ali and the founder of the monarchial dynasty that bears his name gets more in-depth treatment. Askia Mohammed met the fourteenth Abasside caliph of Egypt in 1479, and was conferred with the title, caliph of the black nationalities. He is also legendary for the enormous wealth that he displayed and expended during his visit to the holy city of Mecca when he took with him 1,500 men, and 300,000 pieces of gold, a large portion of which he dispensed within the city and at Medina. He was a staunch Muslim and waged holy wars meant to entrench the reign of Islam, unlike Sonni Ali, who was more restrained in terms of religious fervor. In history, notably Abd al-Sadi's *Tarikh es-Soudan* (The history of the Sudan) (1898/1964), Sonni Ali is portrayed as an uncontrollable tyrant who murdered distinguished scholars and pious men of God alike.

Diop then traces the gradual Islamization of large parts of present-day West Africa, after which he identifies what he considers to be the indigenous structures of rulership:

> Africans ... never experienced a lay republic, even though the regimes were almost everywhere democratic, with a balance of powers. That is why every African is at heart a hidden aristocrat, just as every French bourgeois was before the Revolution. The deeper reflexes of the present-day African are more closely tied to a monarchial regime than to a republican one. Rich or poor, peasant or urbanite, all dream of being a small or great lord rather than a small or great bourgeois. The quality of their gestures and attitudes, their manner of seeing things, whatever their caste, is lordly and aristocratic in contrast to bourgeois "pettiness." (Diop 1987: 72)

In the next line, Diop writes, "there is still one revolution's distance between African and Western consciences, in terms of instinctive behavior" (ibid., 72), a remark that has heavy négritudist tones in its essentializing intents. Diop states that aristocratism was the predominant mode of rulership in Africa generally, and not even its encounter with the West, beginning in the sixteenth century, did much to alter this political characteristic. On the other hand, the encounter with Western civilization leading to eventual colonization halted the internal evolutionary trajectory of African societies, thereby impeding dynamic political initiatives. In places where detribalization had begun to take effect, the trend was reversed, thereby truncating the movement toward political growth and maturity.

Aristocratism and clanism characterized sociopolitical existence in precolonial Africa. After the introduction of modernity, analysts aver that the aristocratism and clanism characterization soon became the primordial and civic dichotomy. So, a bifurcation of the public domain has continued to endure in one form or another. Diop typifies the African as being "an aristocratic collectivist" (ibid., 74), which prevents Africans from attaining a state of "socialist evolution." Further, Diop writes, "the ceremonial of court life was very strict and seem, give or take a few variants, to have been the same throughout black Africa" (79). When in the presence of a monarch, subjects had to sprinkle their heads with dust as a "sign of humility."

In Songhai, during the reign of Askia, the monarchial institution had become thoroughly Islamized. The insignia of the ruler consisted of a seal, a sword, and the Koran, which were claimed to have been granted by the Umayyad of Spain. Scholars of ancient history have attested to Ghana's enormous wealth. The king's headgear was bedecked with gold and other materials of the finest quality; his throne was located inside a pavilion surrounded by horses decorated with gold; his entire entourage was arrayed with the same level of visual splendor consisting of gold and impressive royal paraphernalia.

Ibn Battuta, a Moroccan explorer famously known for his world travels, visited Mali during the reign of Mansa Soleiman in 1351–1353, and found a significant degree of monarchial opulence. In addition, mention is made of "a handkerchief with Egyptian designs" (ibid., 84), which immediately emphasizes the Kemetic links with black Africa.

In examining the ancient monarchies of Ghana, Songhai, and Mali, Diop establishes the presence of powerful territorial kingdoms in Africa, all of which had a significant measure of international standing. In addition, these kingdoms had considerable material wealth, which was displayed and dispensed with internationally. Islam became the predominant religion of the ruling class and the sociopolitical conditions were such that this did not fuel the need for social revolution.

All of these ideas debunk the standard Eurocentric notion of an Africa without history, culture, or civilization. Taken together, this constitutes Diop's work of rebuttal as a classic Afrocentric corpus, an oeuvre of affirmation and agency, of significant and noteworthy black presence, and a rebuttal of severe exclusionary Eurocentrism, which, as substitute for a genuine Africanity, would rather proclaim Africa as at best to be a negation of "universal humanity," and at worst, a cipher. This Diopian articulation of Afrocentricity, which I have termed classical, had to take place between the two polarities – Eurocentrism and extreme Afrocentricity – to be able to make sense of, and confront its most obvious discursive challenges.

Between the tenth and twelfth centuries, the Ghana Empire, which predated the rule of Charlemagne by five hundred years, was the dominant kingdom on the African continent despite significant Berber and Arab presence and all and sundry paid homage and offered tributes to a black emperor. Diop is quite insistent on this point.

Diop makes another significant point regarding the difference in historical trajectories between Western Europe and Africa. Political consciousness and organization in Europe passed through three major stages: the period of the Hellenic city-states, the universality established under the influence of the Church during the Middle Ages, and the construction of modern nation-states, which, it is suggested, became the seedbed of ultra-nationalism and chauvinism. Africa on the other hand, before its encounter with the West, fostered and maintained "universal consciousness" through a commonality of ethics, culture, and material development. Diop also supports the view that African sociopolitical and cultural development did not come from Aryan and Semitic Mediterranean influence, itself, a stance of classic Afrocentricity.

Africa is said to have experienced no mass barbarian invasions as Europe did in the tenth century. Instead, what occurred in Africa was the forceful seizure of North Africa by Arabs. They entered other parts of the continent, notably East Africa, peacefully and became religious leaders and advisors. By virtue of these interactions, collective consciousness was forged and consolidated. This laid the groundwork for continuities in African cultures and traditions. Similarly, there are etymological similarities between the Wolof language and ancient Egyptian, which would explain the connections between the traces of Kemetic modes of rulership in black Africa. This specific claim is crucial to Afrocentric thought.

Another angle central to Afrocentric epistemology is the area of inquiry relating to African cultures of antiquity. The prevailing Eurocentric idea was that Africa was without cultural traditions worth mentioning. However, if literacy is a signifier of cultural development, then it is wrong to assume that Africa had no cultural traditions deserving of notice. Al-Sadi (1898/1964) reported that writing had become an established practice during the Songhai Empire. Askia Musa (second Songhai ruler, 1528–1531), on assuming the reins of power, wrote two letters, one to his mother and the other to his brother. He also wrote about the use of written registers and documents in the Songhai legal system.

Diop makes a telling argument regarding the emergence of capitalism as a world system. He states that for capitalism to develop, there had to be a separation between domestic industry and agriculture. After feudalism reached a crisis provoking widespread unemployment, discontent and mass migrations from rural to urban areas in Europe, capitalism became the only logical alternative. But capitalism being what it is soon exceeded the bounds of its origins, seeking new markets and captives, one of which was Africa. As Diop writes, "expropriation of the sort seen in sixteenth-century Europe was unthinkable in the history of precolonial Africa" (ibid., 150). He further writes: "the end of the Middle Ages and the whole of the Renaissance in Europe were characterized by a degree of slavery as intense as more detestable than what Africa had known" (152).

According to Diop, an erroneous impression persists concerning the question of slavery as a purely African practice. He argues instead that its European manifestation was more entrenched and virulent than what existed in Africa in any form. Slavery was not peculiar to any single race and was practiced generally. However, slavery in Africa worsened progressively after contact with Europe, which abandoned its modes of domestic enslavement and transferred the practice abroad aided by its mastery of more advanced weapons of destruction. Before the encounter with the West, the economy in Africa was characterized by its subsistence nature, in which production never exceeding necessity and hence, nor could create a material culture that radically transformed human existence. Within this context, capitalism was unlikely.

In the religious realm, Diop argues that Islamization in precolonial Africa was not only inevitable was but was also an introduction guided by rationality. Until the reign of the Askias, between the fifteenth and seventeenth centuries (and obviously well after), the practices of libation, offering of sacrifices, geomancy, belief in the Kabbala, and a wide range of manifestations of animism were prevalent in Africa. However, the introduction of Islam is said to have curbed these "unIslamic" practices and standardized the application of religion in everyday life. The processes in which the conversion to Islam occurred involved persuasion, negotiation, and warfare when necessary. Diop states that Islam was more suited to the metaphysical and rational needs of Africa, unlike Christianity, which, in the hands of European invaders, was largely a handmaiden of an overt imperial quest.

Maraboutism is deeply enshrined in Islamic worship in Africa, particularly in the western region. "Marabout" stems from the Arabic el Morabbatin, which means to dwell in a monastery. Within this context, God and his prophet are not approached or consulted without an intermediary in the figure of the marabout. The marabout acts as a go-between between the Almighty and human beings, and is consequently revered by the ordinary faithful, who literally entrust their lives to him. This feature of having an intermediary act between human beings and God dates back to indigenous African modes of worship, in which below God, there is a pantheon of lesser divinities – symbolized by specific cosmic attributes such as the sky, fire, water, and earth – to whom mortals address their entreaties and prayers. These lesser deities also have shrines and priests dedicated to them, unlike for instance Olorun, as the Almighty is known in Yoruba culture. The faithful within Islam were kept in check by the promise of Paradise if an exemplary life is led, on the one hand, or by the spectre of Hell, if deviations from the path of righteousness and religion occur.

Islam was a great source of culture and civilization, as there are great institutions of learning and traditions of Islamic scholarship in Africa. But there was also a pronounced tendency to discard parts of the African past deemed to be unIslamic. As such, large tracts of African collective and institutional memory were lost. Christianity, by contrast, did not institute measures to erase its pre-Christian heritage, and so it is easier to trace the continuities between non-Christian and Christian epochs. Islam classified any non-Islamic inheritance as idolatrous and so the blacks of Khartoum, which is said to be "the Ethiopia of black Africa," viewed their previous links with ancient Meroe (Nubia) with ignominy. Similarly:

> the ruins from that period, the eighty-four pyramids still standing in the ancient capital, the temple of Senna, Meroitic writing, the remains of the astronomical observatories, the vestiges of the metal industry which made the Sudan the Birmingham of antiquity, all this is of no interest because it is tainted with a pagan tradition (ibid., 171–172).

Apart from Maraboutism, Sherifism is another prominent feature of Islam in Africa. Sherifism is the proclivity of Muslim leaders to link their biological ancestry to the Holy Prophet, Muhammad. In making these connections, local history, often altered, becomes subordinate to the overriding conceptual objective. The Muslim faithful, who casted doubt over these far-fetched maneuvers, were pronounced heretical. From the dynasties of Ghana, Bornu, Wadia, and Kodofan, there have been claims tracing religious ancestry and heritage to Yemen in Arabia, with all of them carrying heavy political overtones. Finally, Diop argues:

> Mohammedan black Africa in the Middle Ages was no less original than Christian Europe at the close of antiquity. Both continents were invaded in the same way by alien monotheistic religions which ended up being at the foundation of the entire sociopolitical organization, ruling philosophical thought, and carrying forward intellectual moral values during this whole period. (ibid., 173)

Here, in making his assertion, Diop exercises a degree of caution. Afrocentricity at this juncture does not make cheap triumphalism its major objective: instead, there is a muted yet eloquent call to acknowledge the accomplishments and dignity of Africanity, which within the overriding Eurocentric project are completely ignored, so that Africa becomes a cipher solemnly awaiting its inscription. Here, Afrocentricity is not the bogeyman that it is often labeled to be. Its detractors, without considering its arguments, announce it as myth or failing, by which it becomes a narrow terroristic discourse unworthy of decent intellectual engagement.

However, in spite of the tendency for Muslims in Africa to downplay and ignore their non-Islamic heritage, Arab chroniclers have done a marvelous job of preserving large tracts of the African past, which are always available for further scrutiny and analysis. This past had been erected on solid foundations of Islamic scholarship, in which the Trivium (the study of grammar, Aristotelian logic, and logic) and the Quadrivium (the study of arithmetic, geometry, astronomy, and music) prevailed. Dialecticians, rhetoricians, and jurists all formed part of the general intellectual culture.

In *Primitive Mentality* (1923), Lucien Lévy-Bruhl described primitive peoples as possessing a pre-logical mentality, but in which illustrious intellectual traditions had been established. During the seventh century, the Arabs, who introduced Islamic traditions of scholarship to Africa, were said to be more advanced than the West in the natural sciences. Nonetheless, the Arabo-African regions regressed in certain respects while the West continued to develop its intellectual foundations. Consequently, as Islamic traditions of learning atrophied, the people in the West became *ahlu kitab* (believers in books), which accounts for a sharp rupture in Arabo-African and Western traditions of scholarship. Some accounts mention that the regression of scholarship in black Africa was particularly noticeable between the sixteenth and seventeenth centuries.

Diop believes that future Afrocentric projects should include the recovery of scripts and texts of African antiquity in various vaults in "North Africa, Spain,

Portugal, Egypt, Baghdad, and perhaps even, Chinese annals" (ibid., 182). This effort of recovery would serve to corroborate the astonishing variedness of African civilization prior to colonization and lead to the "resuscitation" as well as "the defossilization of African history" (185). Apart from the noted accomplishments of Islamic scholarship in Africa, it is also worthy of note that there was a hieroglyphic script in Cameroon, which, though of recent historical manifestation, may have a much older origin. There is also the syllabic script of the Vai in Sierra Leone and the Nsibidi alphabetical system of notation. In the realm of art, the brilliance of Ife and Benin sculpture is well known and their classicism has been compared to sixth-century Greek art.

In Afrocentric epistemology, the word is believed to possess magical properties. In ancient Egypt, the Book of Thoth is believed to contain magical incantatory power capable of altering the world. This belief is said to have found its way into Islamic thought and ritual practices and so:

> The recitation of a given verse would allow one to find lost objects, another verse would protect one from his enemies, or from bad luck, and so forth, because the Prophet was supposed to have uttered them in identical circumstances (ibid., 186).

In making talismans, "the theoretically prohibited subject of the Kabbala", (190) passages from the Koran are often employed.

More tangible aspects of Afrocentricity are involved in the validation of claims regarding prehistoric trappings of African material culture. Accordingly, the ruins of the ancient capital of Meroe (Nubia) have been found, based largely on the accounts provided by Herodotus and Diodorus Siculus. Within the architectural ruins of Nilotic Sudan, Carl Richard Lepsius is noted to have found fragments of an astronomical observatory. Also present among the discovered ruins are eighty-four pyramids, which served as royal sepulchers and which are similar those of ancient Egypt. Other notable discovered ruins are the Dzata in Zimbabwe. There have been strong Eurocentric claims asserting that these ruins were probably left by non-Bantu groups such as Persians, Arabs, Phoenicians, or Israelites, but the archaeological excavations made on the sites have produced only Bantoid skeletons.

According to written testimonies of Muslim geographer and historian Al-Bakri (c. 1014–1094), Muslim geographer, cartographer, and Egyptologist Muhammad al-Idrisi (1099–1166), and Moroccan traveler Ibn Battuta, the architectural traditions of precolonial black Africa were also quite developed, with buildings decorated with cupolas and arabesques. The same can also be said about indigenous technologies of bronze casting especially made famous by the remarkable Benin produced artworks which share commonalities with those of the Gulf of Guinea and ancient Meroe. Precolonial African navigational technology has often been debated with some authors commenting on it favorably. There were a few notable disastrous attempts to explore the Atlantic venturing westwards. The Emperor of Mali, Kankan Mussa's predecessor, sent an expedition of two hundred ships into the Atlantic but only one vessel returned. A second expedition was attempted with a contingent of two thousand ships, none of which was said to have returned. Some conjecture advances the view that the ships may have reached America. Leo Weiner documented that Christopher Columbus's noted in his journal that his naval contingent found "black skinned people had come from the south-east in boats, trading in gold-tipped spears" (1920). There was said to be no remarkable antagonism between black Africans and indigenous Americans during the period (Chenqu 2014). In Diop's words, "relations between Africa and pre-Columbian America were relatively constant" (1987: 209).

Having established the characteristics and achievements of precolonial African material culture, Diop then makes some noteworthy claims regarding blacks of antiquity. First, he mentions that Egyptians regarded themselves as coming from the south, specifically Nubia. Also, employing linguistic, ethnological, and toponymic data, he is able to deduce, "after the drying of the Sahara (700 BCE), black mankind first lived in bunches in the Nile Basin before swarming out in successive spurts toward the interior of the continent" (ibid., 213). Applying these research methods, it is possible to trace the origins of nationalities such as the Yoruba, Agni, Serer, and other groups, the Ga, the Gula, the Chari, the Kara, the Kare, the Kipsigi, the Kissi, the Kundu, the Laka, the Nuer, the Sara, the Maka, the Sango, and the Sumba (213–214). What all these African ethnicities share is a common origin in the Nile Valley as "the primitive cradle of all the black peoples today living dispersed at the various points of the continent" (214). Jonathan Olumide Lucas, in his *The Religion of the Yorubas* (1948), claims that the Yoruba of prehistory lived in ancient Egypt, after which they migrated southward, employing similarities in language, religion, and "names of persons, places, and things" (cited in Diop 1987: 216). Exploring this particular trajectory, Lucas establishes that ancient Egyptian deities namely, Osiris, Isis, Horus, Shu, Sut, Thoth, Khepera, Amon, Anu, Khonsu, Khnum, Khopri, Hathor, Sokaris, Ra, and Seb have survived in one form or the other within the Yoruba cultural context. In addition, "[Lucas] reminds us that the ontological notions of ancient Egyptian, such as Ka, Akhu, Ku, Saku, and Ba, are to be found in Yoruba" (217). Similarly, there is a relation between the Egyptian Osiris and Oni, the spiritual and temporal ruler of the ancient Yoruban town of Ile-Ife, which has a nearby hill called Kuse, etymologically similar at least, to Kush in ancient Nubia.

Diop's righteous and appropriate reaction to Eurocentrism led to a most improbable intellectual itinerary; it produced a disciplinary formation that could only have emerged as a response to scientific racism. But having confronted such a pervasive structure of racism, some may argue that his discourse becomes unwittingly tainted by the same brush of racism it so fervently seeks to cast off. In attempting to stamp out an evident evil, his detractors may say that his discourse neglects it because it has to wend its way through a fenced arena of academic language and modes of enunciation. His detractors would be tempted to mention that historical research is often discarded in favor of an ideology of anti-racism. In not reading Diop's project with the great care that it deserves, detractors may say that Afrocentric discourse in his handling substitutes genuine historical research with a mythological African past, which then serves as basis for the present. In this sense, Diop's work connects with, and is similar to the Senghorian concept of négritude from which it strives to distance itself.

Detractors may argue that it is never clear in Diop's numerous generalizations which historical period or part of the continent he is addressing at any particular point in his writing. As such, his methodological assumptions are always suspect. They could say that the coupling of ideology with methodology, in this case, undermines the rigor that his work desperately needs. Afrocentricity serves as a bulwark against Eurocentric racism, which provides it with its raison d'être, after which it begins to falter when subjected to more rigorous scrutiny.

Eurocentric critics may argue that Diop's research methodology is often inadequate, if not obsolete. They may say he begins his analysis of black Africa round 1000 CE, in ancient Ghana, relying mainly on Arab scholars, geographers, and explorers, and that these sources are not subjected to scrutiny along with other similar accounts for accuracy – possibly because they do not exist.

It may be said that Diop has the tendency of essentializing black Africa, a trait often found in ideologies of blackness such as négritude. In addition, Diop's narrative often alludes to the influence of Arabs and Islam in shaping the mores and customs of black Africa, thereby imbuing Afrocentric discourse with undeniable transcontinental attributes.

Could it be said that Diop would rather have us believe that black Africa's modes of political organization were entirely indigenous? This would be generally acceptable by some Eurocentric accounts. Diop himself continually stresses the significance of Arab priests and ambassadors in precolonial black African life, which may grant credence to views that West African divination systems, for instance, bear an evident Islamic derivation. In addition, Africa's modes of indigenous rulership, by certain accounts, display a Buddhist or East Asian derivation, again testifying to a notion of transcontinentality – aligning Africa with other continents – rather than strict autochthony.

In portraying the political, military, economic, and administrative capabilities of black Africa, Diop draws primarily from the ancient empires of Ghana, Mali, and Songhai; his account of Ghana, in some respects, is not as copious as one would have liked it be, but it gets richer as he gets to Songhai, the most recent of the great African empires. This can only mean one thing; reliable knowledge about the other two empires is scarce, with Abd al-Sadi's renowned text, *Tarikh es-Soudan*, supplying much of the information.

Diop invariably finds it necessary to compare African achievements with those of European and Mediterranean regions, which raises an all-too-familiar epistemological issue: the question of the severely racialized Other seeking some existential validation from the dominant category of the Same. This would be the most obvious way to attempt to read this equation. However, Diop is merely attempting to force a conversation that most often does not occur: the improbable dialogue between Afrocentricity and Eurocentrism. The challenge, then, before Afrocentricity, is to transcend the seemingly implacable divide constructed by race that prevents a much-needed conversation, while at the same time fostering a dialectic that reproduces a self-perpetuating violence.

A Eurocentric or reactionary Africanist critique may state that most of Diop's depictions of Africa and foreigners are usually unilateral, in which the former is the passive agent dealing with the obstacles and propositions brought about by external actors. Critics may say that perhaps Diop is not fully aware of the implications of the nature of these exchanges, as Africa tends to be significantly marked by a creeping condition of insularity, always being acted upon as opposed to acting upon the larger world. Such a unilateral position implies a context lacking the desired initiative to engender radical transformation and innovation – cultural, political, economic, and technological. This dimension is, of course, related to the antithetical gulf between the Same and the Other.

Critics may argue that in Diop's wide-ranging account, black Africans almost never venture out of the continent – although this might be a contentious point with the long history of pilgrimages to the holy cities of Arabia – that they always seem to be at the receiving end of a plethora of foreign influences and actors beginning with Islamization and its agents. Diop rightly ascribes the intellectual traditions of precolonial Africa to Islam, which eventually vitiated pre-Islamic roots and sources. The undermining of these vital historical truths – to employ Diop's term – transforms a significant part of Africa's history into a tabula rasa.

Detractors may argue that without really intending it, Diop also ascribes innovative knowledge systems, practices, and institutions in precolonial Africa to foreign factors, thereby supporting the hypothesis that transcontinental continuities are far more important for the development of culture and knowledge than insular identities and mindsets.

On the positive side, it may be said that in *Precolonial Black Africa*, Diop is not really claiming that Africans are the originators of human civilization. Instead, he successfully counters the entrenched beliefs that Africa had no history or culture worth mentioning, that it had no intellectual accomplishments, no discernible levels of humanity and was thus forced to breed within the maw of mindless and endless barbarity. Diop's account is an engaging and eloquent refutation of these obviously erroneous and obsolete notions. But it is also a chronicle of Africa's participation in the dispersal and retention of global knowledge, particularly that relating to technology and material culture. These vital cross-fertilizations have been central through the ages in making Africa what it has become currently and for preserving its traditions.

In Diop's work, the portrait that emerges of the relationship between principally West Africa, ancient Egypt, and Nubia cannot be regarded as tenuous given the presentation of numerous linguistic correlations. Diop is able to demonstrate these connections by tracing the etymologies of common words, names, and corresponding surviving evidence of material culture. Rather than instigating doubt and misplaced curiosity, these provide what ought to be satisfying illumination. Ancient Egypt looms as a site of universal civilization, complete and fully formed. But the role of black Africans in this process is never ambiguous, and cannot be said to be marginal. Indeed, black Africans cannot be said to be the spectral recipients of relics of culture, who are just about to bear testimony to long lost traditions of a dominant cultural configuration. They were central to the dynamics of cultural development and their processes of dispersal.

Apart from the stated etymological similarities to be found between ancient Egypt and black Africa, there are other major connections linking the two regions. The most obvious are durable and convincing elements of material culture, such as architecture, metallurgy, geomancy, and hieroglyphics. Rather than casting doubt on Diop's corpus, this category of evidence ought to cast it in a different light. Diop is often made out to be a reckless scholar rather than a courageous one, and this is probably because opinions are formed about him before actually reading his work.

Diop writes from within the deep injury of racism; he knows intimately its violence, its history, and its utter rejection and denigration of the black subject. As such, a central aspect of his project is to challenge its pervasive oppression, its erasure of the dignity of subject peoples. His project cannot be done justice without due recognition of his ardent response to this ingrained history of injustice. Eurocentrism is not always in a position to recognize and understand the effects and history of this injustice. Even as it perpetrates racism, it has no complete sense of appreciation of its serial modes of victimization, violence, and demoralization. Thus, Eurocentrism is not able to articulate itself from an othered positionality. This incapacity, not unparadoxically, serves as a pure discourse of oppression. So-called scientific truth cannot assuage the injury – psychological and structural oppression – especially when it is allied to the oppressor's campaign. The truth of science when effecting the mandate of oppression is bankrupt, partial, and open to contestation, rigorous query, and perhaps even violence.

Diop's discussion of the ancient empires of Ghana, Mali, and Songhai attests to the significance of African cultures and civilization, which he frequently compares with those of Europe. Africa in this context is not the absolute Other of Europe as it is often claimed but an unfortunate interlocutor that must bear the consequence of the deep violence wreaked on it alone.

Afrocentricity seeks to be more than just an intellectual concept. It is also an ideological confrontation with the deleterious legacies of slavery, colonization, and relentless racial denigration. Indeed, it also serves as the restoration of the collective well-being of a race repeatedly violated and abused by an ideology whose own concept of humanity has always been partial, exclusionary, and based on the violent suppression of others.

Afrocentricity addresses the lingering effects of this prolonged injustice. Eurocentrism can have no redeeming value for Africa as long as it portrays it as fragmentary, severely undeveloped, perpetually marginalized, and forever dependent on foreign influences and inputs. Eurocentrism always seeks to depict Africa as a cipher or a chronically regressive site of anomie.

On the other hand, Diop portrays an Africa of considerable achievements, wealth, vibrancy, and filled with luminous future prospects. There are, as such, no doubts as to where his true sympathies lie. Moreover, Diop is a giant of ideological integrity. He remains a key figure of Afrocentricity because by offering so many well articulated arguments and so much empirical material, he demonstrates why Africa should not be, and cannot be, an object of universal opprobrium and ridicule.

An Afrocentric perspective is one that shows the falsity of notions of African invisibility, marginality, and inferiority. Those who uphold it are constantly seeking to wrest agency and intellectual integrity from a context that is riddled and fractured by hegemony, brutalization, and denigration. Afrocentricity stems from an ingrained reaction to centuries of racial abuse, so, it is sometimes difficult for Eurocentrists to fully comprehend the whys and wherefores of its articulation. In order for Afrocentric discourse to continue to be effective and relevant, the skillful presentation of research findings is paramount. Such material must be carefully assembled and deployed against the corrosive backdrop attesting to centuries of racial violence, which Afrocentricity addresses.

Diop's Afrocentric discourse and positionality were shaped by a specific colonial and racial moment, which had to be confronted by a determined set of responses: the affirmation of the black subject within the continuum of universal history. This is the least Afrocentricity seeks to accomplish. But in the discursive affirmation of an Africanist viewpoint, Diop had to be the spokesman of an entire continent and its diasporas, a task that is almost impossible to avoid just as négritudists were compelled to speak for an Africa effectively concealed from the West. It was within this milieu of contestation and acrimony that classical Afrocentricity took shape; it was a whole-hearted response to a gargantuan existential and intellectual lie, a lie that sought to reduce life to death, a death without boundaries and barriers, in which the black subject had been thrust in perpetuity. Afrocentricity, then, becomes redemption, freedom, and the release of the imaginative spirit. Where silence reigned, it responded in song and speech;

where there was rigor mortis, it rebounded with unrestrained movement. It had to become the antithesis of every category of falsehood and deception that had been pronounced in its name, before it, and in spite of it. It is a lie without limits, a lie that had finally lost the sense of its own immensity and devastating power.

Diop's work operates at least two significant levels: the employment of written Islamic texts to corroborate black life and achievement confers a transcendence that is difficult to shake off the African ontological realm; it also serves as the basis upon which to launch a full-fledged Afrocentric agenda that continues to resonate within the contemporary moment.

The very affirmation of black existence in the face of persistent and prolonged Eurocentric negation establishes the fact that would rather be denied. Here, a joy is released to roam and proclaim its freedom in spite of the woeful history that preceded its birth, a joy without limits and that is sometimes enacted and relived in complete ignorance of its formidable detractors. It is, therefore, a joy that must be crushed because it refuses it acknowledge any masters. Real Afrocentricity is without masters and that is why it is feared, derided, and confronted. When Afrocentricity succeeds, it cannot but proclaim an expansive joy that says, in spite of all, I have not only survived but triumphed. In relation to its opponents, this is an emotion that cannot be tolerated not only because of its arrogant self-sufficiency but also because it denies the artificial truth of its past, a truth that took centuries to diligently fabricate and must now shamefully be consigned to a plume of smoke.

6

Deep Afrocentricity

Molefi Keke Asante is certainly one of the most engaging theorists and advocates of Afrocentricity. It is easy to conclude that his arguments are not granted the degree of attention they deserve, especially by those who refuse to see, or who are unable to gauge the power and hegemony of Eurocentrism. Asante begins his quest to understand phenomena by acknowledging that social science, in its Eurocentric tendency and tradition, fails to recognize that there are other ways of experiencing reality, and that its supposed universality is actually a veneer or a mirage, or perhaps even, something slightly more sinister. As such, most of his work has been to critique Eurocentrism when it is to be found "in the fields of intercultural communication, rhetoric, philosophy, linguistics, psychology, education, anthropology, and history" (Asante 1987: 3).

A large part of Asante's effort is geared toward de-provincializing knowledge production, especially when it designates Africa as object and not as subject. Within the Eurocentric intellectual tradition, Asante views Marxism and Freudism as two sides of the same epistemic coin. As such, he holds that they are only able to offer a truncated version of reality, particularly when it pertains to non-Western cultures. Asante states that he is not against the entire Eurocentric tradition per se, but he is against its claims to universality to the exclusion of all other epistemic traditions. Eurocentric schools of thought such as Marxism and Freudism are "in essence, captives of a peculiar arrogance, the arrogance of not knowing that they do not know what it is that they do not know, yet they speak as if they know what all of us need to know" (ibid., 4). The incorporation of Afrocentric viewpoints would serve to counteract this perceived arrogance.

Against Eurocentrism

Asante seeks to provide a critique of Eurocentric ideologies in their failure to accommodate other conceptions of reality. This intention, in turn, provides the necessity for a counter-paradigmatic project. As such, "Afrocentricity proposed a cultural reconconstruction that incorporates the African perspective as part of an entire human transformation" (ibid., 5). He further elucidates his approach, "the crystallization of this perspective I have named *Afrocentricity*, which means, literally, placing African ideals at the center of any analysis that involves African culture and behavior" (ibid., 6). The limitations of a particular kind of ethnocentrism presenting itself as universal become apparent when it has to transcend its specific culture, society, or environment. Once its attempts to effect this transition, it is revealed as just another instance of precisely what it is, which is a form of ethnocentricism. But very few ethnocentrists are able to acknowledge, let alone confront, the implications of their ideology and unmask what needs to be revealed. Eurocentrism is not merely a trait common to Westerners. As an ideology, it pervades the social sciences, humanities, and critical theory, such that non-Westerners, including Africans and Asians, often mistake it for genuine universality, when, in fact, it ought to be conceived as just a manifestation of what Asante calls "expansive provincialism" (ibid., 7).

Supposedly universal intellectual traditions and ideologies need to be unmasked in order to reveal where their sympathies and interests lie and to elucidate how they are usually situated to strengthen the powerful while at the same time disguising the strategies by which they do so. In the same manner, critics employing a feminist perspective, have criticized social-Darwinist anthropology for its industrial-capitalist orientation, while Marxist analysis has been lauded its more balanced approach to social history and relations. However, Asante does not approve of Marxism as an ideology that ought to be incorporated into the Afrocentric agenda for the reason that it too is derivative of the same parochial Eurocentric tradition that marginalizes and excludes non-Western experiences.

Asante claims that Afrocentricity is characterized by an ethos of inclusiveness, which is contrary to the tendencies inherent in social Darwinism, capitalism, and most versions of Marxist thought. The Eurocentric consciousness is characterized by a false sense of universalism that is supposed to be based on objectivity and historically valid traditions of scholarship. Asante equates the historic Eurocentric appropriation of foreign land – the precursor of colonization – to the total domination of mental consciousness. Indeed, the sequestration of alien territories and the complete subjugation of body and mind were part of a single elaborate imperial project.

In the New World context of the United States, the cultural history and experiences of slaves are discountenanced in favor of the contingencies of a racialized social and economic context, which invents a new concept – the "Negro" as a term to exclude the specificities of history and culture when speaking of Africans whose original spatial and contextual circumstances are ignored in a bid to ascribe to them a different and disconnected rendering of their history.

Eurocentric thought, according to Asante, simply dispenses with African historic realities, which according to the Afrocentric perspective, would entail an espousal of the significance of ancient Kemetic civilization and accomplishments. Similarly, conventional engagements with African-American culture are conducted along the familiar Eurocentric lines that, in Asante' view, impede intercultural communication and understanding as well as devalue humanity. He further adds that the inability to fully connect African-American culture with the African continent, that is, to establish the existential and cultural continuities between Africans in the New World and the Old World, could only lead to gross misrepresentation. The Afrocentric project consequently seeks to redress the lack of dialogue between Eurocentric perspectives and African worldviews.

The Aristotelian invention of inductive and deductive reasoning inaugurated a major characteristic within Western rationality, which Asante considers "reductionist, deterministic and operationist positivist" (ibid., 13). In his view, this approach accounts for the rigid functionalism ascribed to body functions, while the determinism in relation to the universe is derived from the belief that the principles of causation are what govern its operations.

The mind-body dichotomy arose as a result of seventeenth philosophers incorporating the advances in physics, chemistry, and biology to make propositions regarding human nature. Within the context of this intellectual background, materialist thought was inevitable. Asante does not completely condemn the usefulness of materialism, but he advocates the admission of other ways of acquiring knowledge. Scientific knowledge has been touted as the Western civilization's way of transcending parochial and often superstitious systems of belief that are usually in opposition to other communal systems and which enable demagogues and fanatics to inhabit and dominate the knowledge space to the exclusion of the virtues of reason, temperance, order, and justice. But scientific rationality, in its exclusivity, fails to acknowledge the values and possibilities of other ways of knowing that have deepened and enriched human experience and history. Scientific inquiry enforces a demarcation between the processes of discovery and verification and tends to privilege the latter. Asante suspects the value of this rigid division between what ought to complementary aspects of the knowledge making process as it miscasts the challenges involved in the often chaotic journey.

The Theory of Africology

Afrology, (notice the closeness to Nabudere's Afrikology) a term Asante had coined earlier, "denotes the Afrocentric study of African concepts, issues and behaviors" (ibid., 16). The study includes Africans on the African continent and those in diaspora, particularly those in the Americas and West Indies. Areas of attention are "the systematic exploration of relationships, social codes, cultural and commercial customs, and oral traditions and proverbs" (ibid.). In addition, "the interpretation of communicative behaviors, as expressed in discourse, spoken and written, and techniques found in jazz studies and urban street-vernacular signifying" (ibid.) forms part of the research agenda. In seeking to understand the human condition, Afrology recognizes that interactions between feeling (affective), knowing (cognitive) and acting (conative) in knowledge-making processes and procedures. Asante, in amalgamating all three – feeling, knowing, and acting – components of the knowledge-making process, considers his work properly Afrological. In advancing this specific agenda, Asante mentions Wade Nobles, Maulana Karenga, and Leachem Semaj as fellow travelers on the Afrological path.

Nommo, meaning word force, is a concept Asante considers vital to the Afrocentric project. He distinguishes three major rhetorical categories, namely, "Afrocentric-personalism," "Asiocentric-spiritualism," and "Eurocentric materialism." The Eurocentric rhetorical tradition is distinguished by its evident linearity, in which control and regulation are central while the Afrocentric orientation maintains a circularity that signifies a will to interpret and understand rather than to control and predict as is the case with the Eurocentric proclivity. Just as Nabudere believes Western modes of rationality are responsible for the contemporary crisis of epistemology, Asante holds that the dominant Eurocentric conception of reality is flawed in its inability to accommodate other cultural perspectives. Accordingly, Asante goes on to assert that this feature of Eurocentric intellectual traditions is said to have blighted the educative channels of non-Western cultures as true education must not only enlighten but must also be emancipatory.

Similarly, it is possible to tell the effects and power of rhetorical practices and forms. Forensic, deliberative, ceremonial, sermonic, and agitational modes of speech seek to accomplish specific effects. African-American leaders are said to often adopt the sermonic mode of address, since a large proportion of black leaders tend to be religious ministers. Asante posits that these various modes of address embody particular "rhetorical conditions" concerning the "natural context of persons, events, objects, relations, and an exigence that evokes an utterance" (ibid., 23). These different rhetorical conditions, through their specific structures, are susceptible to the stratagems of power. This is most evident in the spheres of religion and politics.

Within the African-American tradition of rhetorical practice, the employment of oratory is vital as can be observed in the special skills of Marcus Garvey, Martin Luther King Jr., Malcolm X, Maulana Karenga, Louis Farrakhan, and Jesse Jackson (ibid., 26). The speaker and his/her audience are involved a hierarchical relationship that is further structured and determined by what is termed "the architectonic industrial-political-technical environment" (ibid.). The speaker's message is expected to be wholesome while seeking to accomplish its intended effect. Societal conditions ordinarily ought to determine the range of effects a speaker may achieve, which is not expected to subvert the sociopolitical and cultural order whether under capitalist or socialist ideology.

However, African-Americans have always been compelled to resist the ideologies of the dominant political elites because of the prolonged history of violence, marginalization, and dispossession to which they have been subjected. So, within the context of the environment in which an embedded rhetorical engagement occurs, there is, on the one hand, a relationship with the speaker, and on the other, a relationship with the sociopolitical milieu, one that is formed and fueled by resistance. For instance, a terrorist regime may disguise the devastation of its terror while at the same time eliciting support for itself, thereby further extending its power. In relation to its victims who are its subjects, it prevents the possibility of an alternative choice as it has managed to impose an order that entrenches its particular vision of the world. This occurred, for example, during the period of apartheid in South Africa, when some of its Western supporters campaigned against the inauguration of democracy in the country.

Part of the way in which a hegemonic order exercises power is the manner in which language is employed to denigrate and demoralize its victims. Furthermore, it constrains the possibilities to discover formal channels to vent resistance, and so, it is able to perpetuate its utter domination of the sociopolitical space in both symbolic and structural terms. As such, a speaker working in support of Eurocentric ideology within a Eurocentric environment is able to formulate a discourse of considerable potency simply because of the pre-existing empowering structures and conditions.

The hegemonic order constrains the ways and possibilities for acquiring knowledge. Furthermore, it defines what constitutes knowledge. Some have claimed that rationalism and empiricism, even though they are established approaches in epistemology, ought not be considered the only avenues for gaining knowledge. They point to the fact that mystical forms of knowing and other related esoteric traditions should also constitute accepted approaches to acquiring knowledge.

Rationalism often articulates and presents itself as an incontestable sign of universality, a benchmark established by reason in the strictest impartiality over and above history, culture, and time. It is also employed by hegemonic powers to further entrench themselves. So, for instance, when there were agitations for the establishment of departments of Black Studies in the United States, the students concerned had to adopt innovative strategies to not only ensure that their messages would be channeled through the appropriate routes, but they also had to seek to alter the prevailing structural and symbolic environment in which they were received and assessed. In other words, their discourse not only had to accomplish a transformative effect on its audience but it also had to alter the unequal hierarchical structure of the intended environment, thereby exposing it for what it truly was, a disempowering tyrannical entity that was unheeding and ruthless toward its victims. If this inherent unequal hierarchical structure and its relations are not transformed, victims of its violence would never be truly free and may in fact become acquiescent with the dominant order in their own victimization. In order to avoid this situation, Asante recommends the development of "an ample metatheory ... founded Afrocentric bases" (ibid., 32).

This Afrocentric metatheory would, of course, contest the Western philosophical tradition, which has been characterized as "a series of footnotes to Plato" (Alfred North Whitehead cited in Asante 1987: 33). However, these footnotes ended up providing the rationale for Eurocentric hegemony, which prides itself as being founded on the basis of the pure rationality of ancient Greece. Thus, Sophocles becomes the exemplar of comedies and tragedies; Greek sculpture is then considered the apogee of artistic perfection; Herodotus and Thucydides are regarded as historians par excellence; Homer becomes the standard bearer for bards engaged in epic poetry; and Plato and Aristotle are crowned as the ultimate rhetoricians. In short, the whole of ancient Greek culture and civilization are anointed the most accomplished ever seen.

In order to contest this Eurocentric domination of global intellectual culture, Asante advocates nothing short of a "post-Western or meta-Western metatheory" (ibid., 34) filtered through an Afrocentric prism. The failure to achieve this mission could only lead to more misunderstanding and misrepresentation. Asante narrates a case in point regarding the work of Isidore Okpewho, the Nigerian scholar. Okpewho had attempted to offer a structuralist interpretation of the Ijaw foundational myth of Woyengi, which, in Asante's view, fails miserably because Claude Lévi-Strauss's theory could not account for the "dynamic, polyvalent mythic possibilities that are meta-Western" (ibid., 97) and instead the entire scholarly effort is encumbered by strictures and presuppositions that fail to yield adequate understanding.

Furthermore, Asante claims that a cultural malady "afflicts a whole generation of thinkers and artists encapsulated by European cultural domination" (ibid., 103). In order to accomplish the flourishing of Afrocentric initiatives and perspectives, it is important to note that creativity and innovation within the Afrocentric consciousness can only come about when agency is articulated and actualized outside the parameters set by Eurocentric frameworks.

Word Force

The efficacy of a metatheory does not reside in its clearly defined functionality but in its malleability and its potentials for enlargement. Asante bestows a lot of importance on nommo as word force, and this is reflected in his focus on Ebonics, "the prototypical language of African Americans" which is "a composite of *ebony and phonetics*" (ibid., 35). The application of language within this context is not predicated on science but instead is regarded as an inventive skill in the possession of a user. In the employment of language, speakers embark upon a search for structure and harmony, which transports them into the unknown. Asante elaborates on the notion of metatheory:

> The constituents of the metatheory *are frame of mind, scope of context, structure of code, and delivery of message.* This fundamental analytical system allows us to be open to the infinite potentialities of communication, and the constituents of this metatheory aid us in determining the innovations in African American communicative behavior without an undue concentration on either grammatical, syntactical, semantic or lexical components. (ibid., 36)

The study of the rhetorical culture of African-Americans is particularly interesting. Linguists have noted that some African-American speech patterns reflect phonological and morphological patterns derived from African roots. Thus, this inflects their rhetorical traditions with some highly distinctive markers. For instance, the lyrical deportment of African-American preachers is well known and this distinction can be said to have pervaded the entire culture.

Asante enumerates some features that characterize African-American language, namely, the value of humanism, the value of communalism, the feature of oppression and paranoia, the value of empathetic understanding, the value of rhythm, the principle of limited reward and, the principle of styling (ibid., 37). He is particularly interested in issues of rhythm and styling, by which a speaker creates cadences, resonances, and uncommon effects. These could come about as a result of well-timed pauses, the imaginative use of the voice and tonal inflections, and the specific circuits through which the message is filtered. All these rhetorical devices are intended for particular effects just as the question of "sounding good" is a much-cherished trope and aim of black speech.

The involvement of the audience is also important in seeking to make a speaker sound good because it prescribes the parameters through which a speech acquires the vibrancy of form and substance. As such, a speech is treated as a living organism nurtured by breath, cadence, and imagination. Without these factors, speech would remain flat, lifeless, and disconnected from its audience, which, rather than receiving verbal nourishment and energy, would feel disembodied and somewhat disenfranchised. For a speech in its inactivated state to accomplish the activation of its meaning and a vibrant form, a set of relations between speaker, message, and audience has to be established. Asante also mentions the importance of visual styling for a speaker to attain the desired effect. The visual is transformed into a metaphor to be manipulated to achieve intended goals. Words are invoked for their emotive power; without the infusion of subjectivity, cadence, and imagination, content and substance hang in abeyance without anchors.

The experience of slavery and racial denigration has had a tremendous impact on black communicative patterns and behavior. Asante points out that the rhetorical practices of African-Americans are characterized by lyricism and poeticism, which are progressively lost as one moves away from the community. The oral traditions of African-Americans are important, since they provide the lyrical basis for speech. Orality is also vital because, knowledge, history, and culture within the African-American community were transmitted from generation to generation by oral means and not written texts until perhaps the twentieth century. Not only were oral traditions a vital historical, intellectual, and cultural resource, they were also an unbreakable link between the present and a living past that has continued to define and animate the present. And so, if words were the keys to the mosaic of the past, they had to be endowed with character, omniscience, and transcendence; otherwise, they would lose their power and significance within an engaged and engaging context of orature.

Thus, Asante affirms, "Africa is at the heart of *all* African-American behavior. Communication styles are reflective of the internal mythic clock, the epic memory, the psychic strain of Africa in our spirits" (ibid., 48). He extends this line of thought to the power of the voice to compel, conjure, and transform, similar to the casting of spells. The voice, like words, has to be imbued with subjectivity and emotiveness to further elevate the force of meaning. Thus, one understands that voice, much like the calimba, Fontomfrom, or flute, is an instrument for the conveying of ideas. When one speaks of the orator, it is necessary to see that, in African culture, voice is an instrument just as significant as the lexical items spoken (ibid.).

This brings us back to the concept of nommo, which is about the power and magic of the word to invoke, as well as transfigure, that which falls under its spell. Asante observes the manner in which contemporary African-American disc jockeys attempt to invoke the incantatory spell of words in their line of work. Here, the widespread notion of "the signifying monkey" (see Gates 1988) is granted even greater resonance.

The employment of words within the context of dispossession and powerlessness can accomplish unexpected effects; in their invocatory and fully charged mode, they possess the capacity to reconfigure social order to the benefit of the disenfranchised. Speakers using their skill with words are able to create a different reality from the apparent one. In African and African-American cultures, words remain mere words until animated by rhythm, stylization, and form; then they are able to attain full incantatory power. A speaker versed in traditions of African oratory knows best not to approach the subject in question directly; *indirection* is considered a vital method. It is necessary to skirt issues, create verbal feints, use strategically placed pauses, and dissimulation before one gets to the point. Attempting to get to the point without method and strategy leads to a vitiation of both form and substance. Scholars have noted that the devastation of slavery has not caused a cessation of the method of indirection amongst African-Americans, a method that had been implanted in the collective psyche before slavery times. Apart from serving to conjure the evocative power of words, the method of indirection is also a means of protection, that is, a way of concealing information that might be detrimental to one's self.

African-American rhetorical traditions are also marked with a great deal of improvisation, as is to be expected given the fact that words have to evoked, prompted, and cajoled. In doing this, they come alive with fire and force, and the techniques by which this magical state is attained are not necessarily procedural. Instead, the ability to call forth the power of words depends on the skills and imagination of the speaker. As such, impromptu, conversational, and extemporaneous modes of address are common with African-American orators, as these forms leave speakers with ample room to explore their improvisatory prowess.

For the success of an improvisatory speech act, the timing of the speaker is essential, just as gauging the conditions of the environment, such as when or when not to be exact. As Asante states, "just as with jazz, which is the classical music of America, the improvised voice, with spontaneity and variety, is the voice of African American oratory" (1987: 54). He adds that there is a diversity of styles and rhetorical strategies available to the Afrocentric orator, which are drawn directly from African-American culture and which are quite distinct from white rhetorical traditions:

> the Afrocentric presentation forms are related to music, particularly the epic styles of blues and jazz. The forms may be seen further back, in the work songs, which predate the blues, spirituals, and jazz. In these folk-forms one finds the call-and-response, improvisation, and rhythm. (ibid., 54–55)

Asante then makes a very significant assertion concerning the whole symbol essence and implications of language. Language, in his view, is not an impartial, neutral property, but invested with history, culture, and substantial communal heritage. Considered in this light, it provides the grounds for the whole articulation of the memories, fears, triumphs, and aspirations of a community. If it is unable to do so, it becomes a sterile property detached from the community, one that stifles its history, culture, and imagination. According to Asante, America enforces a monoethnic conception of language in a multiethnic context to the disadvantage of ethnic and racial minorities.

The use of pejorative terms such as *"blackball," "blackmail," "black Friday"* etc. (ibid., 55) foists a particular concrete as well as symbolic identification of language that fails to present the whole cultural, linguistic, ethnic, and racial situation existing in America. It is really a distorted and degraded picture of the multiethnic context of the United States. The power of "symbol imperialism" is therefore considered more devastating than institutional racism as they are more subtle and work directly on subconscious states.

Symbol imperialism pervades many multi-ethnic contexts dominated by Eurocentric ideology in the form "'flesh'-colored Band-Aids, traditional American combs, sunglasses or regular eyeglasses, or the nude look – all of which disregard racial variations in skin color and bone structure" (ibid., 56). Non-white communities and groups are then forced to play "catch up" in such societies. This form of symbol imperialism extends to contemporary Eurocentric intellectual culture, in which the Jungian notion of archetypes or the structuralist mode of analysis pioneered by Levi-Strauss are considered universal models to be applied without restriction or qualification when in fact they are culturally specific.

The debate about the advantages and disadvantages of Ebonics in the United States is related to the issue of fostering a monocultural conception of language upon a multiethnic situation. According to an Afrocentric point of view, Ebonics is a creative linguistic response to a highly racialized and exclusionary environment. However, those intent upon maintaining the white power structure view it as a "non-standard" instrumentalization of language that has no grounding in logic, order, or "accepted" linguistic practice. From an Afrocentric perspective, nothing could be more fallacious. Ebonics, according to the Afrocentric perspective "was a creative enterprise, out of the materials of interrelationships and the energies of the African ancestral past" (ibid., 57).

Emancipation, in a Eurocentric context, is an all-encompassing project that involves the transformation of concrete and symbolic structures. This expression does not capture all the dimensions, but hopefully it refers to the visible and invisible aspects of transformation. Even when speaking about "freedom" and "liberty" in a Eurocentric environment, it is important to note these terms are couched with a specific historical understanding based on exclusivity and exclusion. In other words, it upholds and reserves the right to liberty for a particular group of people while at the same time denying it to others and not managing to see the contradiction in this quixotic equation. Prevailing Eurocentric ideology and structures rarely succeed in reflecting the knowledge systems and traditions of marginalized communities because they are unwilling or "unable" accommodate anything beyond the ideals of their heritage.

Africa as Teacher

In order to understand Africa's concept of communication, Asante delves into the African ancestral past and discovers that "there is vocal-expressive modality that dominates all communication culture" (ibid., 59). So, he mentions that apart from the ancient kingdoms of Meroe, Kemet, and Abyssinia, textuality was hardly the norm in other parts of Africa. The drum was an instrument of communication, in which messages were related from drummer to drummer over wide distances until they reached their intended audiences. Village drummers and sages were regarded as custodians of history and collective memory.

Asante establishes a sharp demarcation between the written word and the spoken word: spoken vs. written. The spoken word is imbued with life and vibrancy and its significance as a "connecting tissue" between being and existence was carried along by Africans coming into the New World. Within African-American culture, the spoken word is often accompanied and embellished by dance and music; better still, within the spoken word itself are dance and music through which its signals its presence, glory and efficacy. Asante considers this phenomenon worthy of study by itself, and hence, within the concept of "orature," he includes, "the sum total of oral tradition, which includes vocality, drumming, storytelling, praise singing, and naming" (60) under the rubric of Pio Zirimu's term "orature."

In spite of the African penchant for the full activation of the spoken word, writing systems did exist in Africa, such as evinced by the Kemetic *Book of the Dead*; the Nsibidi, which is a system of writing developed by the Efik; and the Adinkra symbols, an ideographic writing system established by the Asante. There are other examples, such as the sacred Benin art symbols associated with the Oba of Benin and the Bamum syllabary, most of which Asante claims developed independent of Eurocentric influence. The limited spread and impact of these various writing systems is possibly due to the fact that they were usually restricted to the priestly and aristocratic elites. Ideographic systems were employed to transmit knowledge about "manhood or womanhood, agriculture, circumcision, astronomy, geometry, healing and ethics" (ibid., 61).

Nsibidi, in particular has been studied in some detail. It has been discovered that, along with other similar African writing systems, it bears some remembrance to ancient Egyptian writing technology. Nsibidi later re-emerged in Cuba as *anaforuana* and as *veve* in Haiti, with the slave trade acting as the most probable channel of the transmission.

Asante makes some claims regarding ancient African cultures that need further substantiation. One claim is, "humans who interact vocally with others for the purpose of achieving cooperation have certainly existed in Africa much longer than in Europe or Asia" (ibid., 62). Archaeological or anthropological evidence is not provided to support this assertion.

However, he makes convincing claims concerning the difference between Eurocentric and Afrocentric philosophical outlooks. First of all, it is important to note that a community's cosmological disposition is largely determined by the founding and lingering myths that constitute its historical realities. In addition, its natural environment goes a long way in shaping what its major behavioral patterns will be. For example, it has been hypothesized that living in temperate regions encourages a siege mentality, social and personal withdrawal, fierce survivalism, and xenophobia, while life in tropical regions breeds sociability, and communal rites such elaborate burials, ancestor worship, and general openness.

Asante goes on to claim that "African society is essentially a society of harmonies, inasmuch as the coherence or compatibility of persons, things, and modalities is at the root of traditional African philosophy" (65).

African rhetorical traditions, are then said to be characterized by the quest for harmony and stability, in which confrontation and discord are avoided. Asante singles out the practice of libation among the Ga of West Africa in order to buttress his point. Ordinarily, libators are poets of note, often with a shamanic disposition. They are expected to be versed in the cultural history and traditions of the people and this is reflected when they hold court. Employing poetic skills, the libator refers to history, culture, and myth to inspire and elevate the audience while imparting the message. The message is more than a mere message in the strict sense of the word because the libator is employing rhetorical skills to build bridges between the present and the past, the present and the future, and ultimately, between the living and the dead. All of this is expected during the act of libation. In Asante's words:

> libation, one of the purest forms of African word magic combines all elements of structure, style, invention, generation, and the productive capacity of sound that are found in the best African oratory. (ibid., 68–69)

Thus, within traditional African philosophy, sound is regarded as being evocative and mystically powerful. Accordingly, "the word is productive and imperative, calling forth and commanding" (ibid., 69). Asante elaborates further:

> the word is imperative, it is the fundamentals well as the fashioning instrument of traditional African society. All religion, music, medicine, and dance are produced by vocal expression, inasmuch as creativity is called into existence by man speaking. There is also a correlation between the effectiveness of the word and the power of the speaker as expressed by his personality and status. The more powerful the priest, the stronger his incantations and invocations. But no priest can exist apart from the word; indeed, without the word, nothing can be, for the word creates reality. (ibid., 70)

The spoken word is a source of power, a connective bond within the community, a musical and therapeutic instrument to mend broken relationships and aspire to the transcendent, a way of communicating with the dead, a tool for invoking the presence of ancestors, in short, a bridge through which the community moves between the finite and the infinite in its perennial search for cosmic and existential harmony.

Some of the assertions Asante makes would undoubtedly appear to the Eurocentric mindset as marred by undue essentialization, for example:

> unlike the Euro-American, the African seeks the totality of an experience, concept, or system. Traditional African society looked for unity of the whole rather than specifics of the whole; such a concentration contributed to community stability

because considerations in the whole were more productive than considerations in detail. (ibid., 79)

The success of public discourse is predicated on three main factors: the logical organization of a speech, the ability for it to enchant and finally, and the amount of word force it is able to conjure. Logical sequencing is not what decrees the success or failure of a speech. Much more than that, the ability of a speaker to discover the hidden power and energy behind images, to strike a chord that resonates with an audience, or, in the traditional setting of a community, guarantees the degree of impact the speaker is able to exert. Bringing a speech to life is a performative event based largely on the skills and imagination of a speaker and the degree of effectiveness of the speech in transporting an audience.

Asante argues that in the traditional African context, the speaker does not adopt the sterile role of a detached lecturer. Instead the speaker seeks to be a poet; the speaker is expected to be able to enchant and transport through the gift of poetry. The ability to uplift an audience with an evocative assemblage of powerful verbal imagery, history and culture is what distinguishes talented African and African- American orators. Thus, where communal bonds are fractured, they mend; where lost spirits loiter outside the fringes of the community, they retrieve and heal through the power of words; when hope is extinguished by despondency, they reset it alight; and when communication with the ancestors has been broken, they re- establish contact. To be sure, this is more than a logical presentation in the narrow sense. The speaker seeks to constantly rebuild the community through vivid and evocative oratorical skills.

Apart from the obvious influence of their African heritage, African-Americans were compelled by their environment to rediscover and consolidate the power of the spoken word simply because slaves were proscribed from learning and writing in English. As such, the issue of word force came to assume an even greater importance in the communicative culture of the community. Once again, Asante emphasizes the importance of orature as, "the comprehensive body of oral discourse on every subject and in every genre of expression produced by people of African descent. It includes sermons, lectures, raps, the dozen, poetry, and humor" and it is distinguished from "oratory," which is "the practice of eloquent public speaking" (ibid., 84).

During slavery times, even when Africans in the New World were denied the means to Western education, they carried along the seeds of a fertile oral tradition, which they capitalized upon to sustain them through times of material deprivation and hardship. Viewing the spoken word as possessing therapeutic properties and transformative effects, they were able to create imaginary worlds of freedom and dignity, which were needed to endure the violence, injustice, and degradation of their actual realities. As those realities constantly sought to demean and extinguish life, the spoken word emerged as a life-affirming force bearing hope and comfort.

On plantations, as Africans toiled under relentless heat and thirst, the songs they sang nourished and strengthened them. The spoken word is thus a bearer of life even under circumstances when actual death was prominent and proclaimed.

In the American context during the tribulations of slavery, the power of the spoken word as employed by Africans as a buttress against the ravages of their plight does not stem from the appropriate grammatical use of language, perfect elocution, or lexical structures. By themselves, they are not generative of transformative verbal essence or vitality. The evocative power of the spoken word comes from the rhythmic employment of sound as a transformative and emotive force. One discovers the hidden force within an imaginative deployment of the spoken word, which then acts as a transfigurative and life-enhancing element. Without this discovery of the life force of the spoken word, it remains lifeless and flat and incapable of enacting its transformative potential. In the United States, the heritage of African concept of nommo enabled African-Americans to invent an alternate tradition of communicative behavior that reflected their particular circumstance which was quite distinct from what existed in the mainstream. The mainstream had excluded them together with their culture and history. But they were able to sustain their oral traditions which paved the way for the emergence of a remarkable parallel world that would eventually be to the benefit of the United States in its entirety and the rest of the world.

Asante writes; "the scholar, rhetorician, or historian who undertakes an analysis of the black past without recognizing the significance of vocal expression as a transformative agent is treading on intellectual quicksand" (ibid., 86). He mentions that African-American leaders are usually formidable orators and not mere intellectuals, no matter their accomplishments as thinkers. Black American leaders were usually masters of the spoken word because it is an instrument of potency and transformation that cemented the community while at the same time possessing the seeming ability to transcend it. Black leaders recognized this and had to capitalize on it to secure their standing within the community. They were transformed by their possession of the word just as they succeeded in transforming their community.

Indeed, no one is immune to the power of the spoken word. The relation between a speaker and an audience is an event. For it to be regarded as successful, it must be completely interactive. The interactive event is characterized by antiphony, enacted via an adept combination of subject matter, theme, and rhythmic structure. Antiphony is an approach that originated in Africa and was transplanted into African-American music and rhetorical behavior.

We are not to underestimate the dominance of Eurocentric ideology, which, for instance, has even infiltrated the sacred African practice of naming. Accordingly, the only means by which a black subject attains dignity and self-recognition is by resistance; resistance affirms a definite articulation of identity in the midst of enforced disintegration. The environment, necessarily hostile, promotes an identity suited to the expectations of the racial ruling elites, one that has no bearing on, or consideration for, the specificities of the black subject.

Asante enunciates perhaps the most important motif of the Afrocentric project, which is how Africans, as victims of slavery, were to come to terms with the abominable injustice that it was. How were they to confront its reverberations that continue to linger even after liberation? How were they to recover their pre- slavery consciousness and orientation under conditions that sought to permanently sever them from an unsoiled heritage? These questions constitute a distinctive problematic that has made Afrocentricity an important project, in Asante's view, for all peoples of African descent and which is certain to ensure its continuing relevance. In the same vein, he continues:

> What is more demonstrative of a people's proud heritage than the pre-American values and attitudes of Africans? When the Yoruba, Fanti, Efik, Congo, Asante, Dahomeans, and Mandingo arrived in America, they had no past of family instability, disrespect for elders, and juvenile insurrection. So, when the contemporary warrior- orators express the belief that white racism has been the chief obstacle to black psychological and physical liberation, they are speaking of the central position of slavery in our history. They are taking an anti-apartheid, antislavery, antiracist position and are becoming in the process the embodiment of resistance. It is this psychological-political resistance that constitutes a universe of alternative discourse (ibid., 87).

More than merely constituting "a universe of alternative discourse," the precolonial African heritage provides Afrocentricity with the machinery for its rationale, one which becomes immediately global in its breadth and one whose conceptual impetus and apparatus link the past together with the present and the future. Framed in this manner, the Afrocentric project secures its relevance and legacy even before it has completed its journey, and this is a journey that will continue as long as racism exists to remind its victims of how the scourge was confronted and resisted by its primary opponents (Africans).

Messianism, Redemption, and the Return

The initial African-American orators, who were often trained in seminaries, took whatever they found useful for public speaking and deliberation – phonetics, exegesis, and homiletics – coupled with the practical actualization of the concept of nommo (transmitted through their African heritage), which transformed the apparently simple act of public speaking into intense collective events as to be expected when the power of the spoken word was realized and incorporated in African rites of communal engagement.

Messianism is often associated with African-American orators in the manner in which hope and transcendence were invoked over the unbearable travails of a racialized present. As such, themes of deliverance and redemption became recurrent; a heavily oppressed people were expected to be freed from the yoke of oppression. The African-American form of messianism placed fervent hopes on the appearance of black saints, who would not only deliver their people from the burden of oppression but would also go on to save the world. In time, Asante asserts, this strand of messianic rhetoric would cause contradictions in the antislavery movement, in which black orators came to be perceived as reactionaries, while white Friends were regarded as the real revolutionaries behind the antislavery effort. Asante disagrees with this view and instead alludes to the crucial work of black orators. After the formal abolition of slavery, Marcus Garvey, who "possessed an awesome combination of force and form to electrify millions" (ibid., 91) continued with the fight for racial equity. Asante continues, "[Garvey's] bombastic oratorical performances, played out with sensitive and dramatic understanding of a cultural phenomenon, made him the most widely acclaimed black spokesman of any generation" (ibid.).

The complexity of speech and thought is very much evident in traditional African thought. Marcel Griaule, an ethnologist studied the Dogon of Mali for several years, attempting to understand a very elaborate cosmological and metaphysical system. He had the opportunity to listen to Ogotemmêli, a renowned Dogon priest and hunter. For thirty-three days, Ogotemmêli expounded on the myths, history, and culture of the Dogon employing a language that was by turns "elaborate, symbolic, and eloquent" (see Griaule 1965). Griaule had to study the culture for sixteen years before he could gain some understanding of it and what he eventually learned was that were four stages to knowledge; notably, the word at face value, the word off to the side, the word from behind, and the clear word (Asante 1987: 94). Furthermore, there are eight levels of the clear word, the knowledge of which was reserved for only the most accomplished and gifted priests. Asante points out the correlation between Africans in the United States and in Africa: "African American thought, as expressed in religion and myth, may be seen as extension of the African foundations" (95).

Another continuity between African and African-American cultures is the central role myth plays in both. Myths are regarded as ways and sources of preserving culture and history, emphasizing the connection between humankind and nature, and finally, re-enacting the belief in the power of the spoken word. In both Africa and black America, the preservation of mythological beliefs and systems is usually left to elders within the community. The belief in myth, apart from emphasizing the link between humankind and nature, celebrates the connection between the living and the dead.

Ancestor veneration is common in both cultures, particularly on the continent of Africa. Asante says that libation is still practiced in the southern parts of the United States.

However, Asante stresses that a noted distinction in the belief in myth in black America is "the demonstration of control over circumstances, as opposed to control over nature" (ibid., 100). In addition, he adds that African-American myths "possess a kind of epistemological maturity, unlike the traditional African myth, which may be seen as an interpretation of reality" (101).

What probably accounts for this supposed "epistemological maturity" is the African-American location within a Euro-American framework, in which both the technologization and desacralization of ordinary life are regarded as indices of progress. In addition, the origins of African-American myth lie in the tragedy of slavery and the protracted struggle against it. It rose out of the experience of modernity and this provides reason for its immediacy, embeddedness, and discernible location in recent memory. Asante is convincing when he states that "contemporary African-American myth contains the powerful suffering genre" (ibid., 103). Associated with extreme suffering and degradation is the ability to convert its negativity into an ethics of a higher level, in which the affliction and suffering become the vehicle that ultimately cleanses and redeems the world.

Asante directs attention to Harriet Tubman, the phenomenal crusader against slavery, who delivered over three hundred slaves to freedom during the height of its oppression. Tubman has assumed mythical proportions in being able to transcend a seemingly insurmountable obstacle with her dignity and humanity intact. She becomes a tireless maternal giver who never fails to put her community first and by so doing, earns its undying admiration and veneration.

Asante makes a highly noteworthy point saying, "within the Afrocentric culture one sees a distaste for individual achievement that is not related to collective advancement" (ibid., 105). This communal ethos is discernible in extended family structures and philanthropy aimed at community building, the poor and the infirm within the community, and a host of diverse church activities. Heroic myths play a vital role in black America and there is a plethora of heroes and heroines whose stature has assumed mythical proportions beginning with John Henry, Stagolee, Shine, John Jasper, and the aforementioned Harriet Tubman. John Henry stands for incredible physical energy and endurance. Such was what was deemed necessary to overcome the enormous challenges and unremitting oppression faced by African-Americans. Stagolee stands for unsullied individuality and independence and a maverick quest to attain personal distinction in midst of spirit-crushing obstacles. But more than just embodying the myth of irresistible individual singularity, Stagolee is identified thus:

> the prototype bad man in the sense that nobody bothered him, not even the devil. He is the embodiment of a myth that emphasizes toughness. Known for his supranatural skill at surviving the worst personal tragedy and emerging victoriously, Stagolee is the ultimate projection of the black phallus into the white belly of America. (ibid., 106)

Perhaps even more than causing considerable discomfort for mainstream America, Stagolee stands for unyielding resistance to the forces that seek to decree black life inconsequential and invisible. So rather than submit to this existential reduction and erasure, black existence needs to constantly affirm its presence and validity and so when mainstream society demanded silence from it, the African-American community screamed out the reality that was itself. It had no need to heed the injunctions of white America since it had been ignored and disrespected at every turn. Resistance is not merely articulated to counter the injustices of mainstream society, it became also an implement for collective affirmation; resistance gave the lie to the intended plan of social relegation and emasculation. Thus, it went beyond the stance of resistance for its own sake; resistance became a necessary strategy for collective survival. Thus, behavior that was merely considered "wild, outrageous, hostile and antisocial" (ibid., 108) actually stood for a potent and cogent denunciation of the entire sociopolitical edifice that sought to strip black America of its strength, creativity, dignity, and agency; in short one that intended to reduce it to a vegetative state. The myth of Stagolee embodies resistance that is well-conceived and necessary and so it can be concluded that "Stagolee is the myth that allows the African American to rail against evil with violence, to shoot, to cut, to maim, to kill – if that is necessary to restore a sense of human dignity" (ibid.).

In order for the rhetoric of resistance to be truly effective and emancipatory, it is necessary to discover a new vocabulary loaded with fresh symbols, imagery, and accents. Frantz Fanon had anticipated the problem of the oppressed after gaining freedom, adopting the language of the oppressor. This is a postcolonial tragedy that has unfortunately become so pervasive. If the oppressed are to attain the height of their creative potentials, they must invent a new language other than that bequeathed to them by the oppressors. According to Asante; "to speak the same language means that you will always be at a disadvantage, because the oppressed can never use the language of the established order with a much skill as the establishment" (ibid., 114–115). He continues; "To speak the same language as the oppressor does not lead to a positive result. To introduce new ground is the method to achieve the extreme dimensions of the protest medium" (115).

In Asante's view, black rhetoric in America is considered problematic in terms of its accessibility to non-speakers of the form. However, he attributes this inaccessibility to the climate in which it took shape, characterized as it was by the antagonism between slave and master, and further fueled by mutual distrust, hatred, and hostility. As such, the form had to exclude those who were considered enemies. There is a difference between when black rhetorical patterns are enacted before a white audience and when they were directed at a black one. Before a black audience, black rhetoric is said to reflect a pronounced lyricism that draws heavily upon its sermonic heritage. For a white audience, this rhetorical approach would be regarded as "being too black." However, to a black audience, the way it would be delivered would likely be deemed too staid and constricted. In the same manner, "there is an overwhelming opposition to the black cultural style of speech by white audiences, who see politicians more as technicians and less as moral persuaders" (117). Ultimately, black rhetoric is shaped by the peculiar experiences, history, and culture of African-Americans which differ markedly from those of white Americans.

However, it is not easy for black subjects to maintain an unalloyed or uninfluenced conception of their identity. It is more than likely that, just as any other life- transforming event such birth, maturity, and death, the black person is certain, at one point or the other, to confront the challenge of "double-consciousness." Double-consciousness arises from the contradictions of existing in two different – and perhaps antagonistic – cultural and ontological frameworks. As defined by W. E. B. Dubois:

> this sense of always looking at one's self through the eyes of others, of measuring one's soul by the tape of a world that looks on in amused contempt and pity. One ever feels his twoness, – an American, a Negro; two souls, two thoughts, two unreconciled strivings; two warring ideals in one dark body, whose dogged strength alone keeps it from being torn asunder. (2008: 12).

Within the American context, double-consciousness becomes acute when one needs to define oneself through the mirror of "another" (in this case, racial other) thereby leading to the emergence of a skewed consciousness. So powerful was this phenomenon that even Dubois, a noted advocate for black empowerment, did not possess cultural and contextual wherewithal to contest and overcome some of the intrusions of Eurocentric ideology made into his outlook. Asante claims that Dubois … was not an Afrocentricist; he was, preeminently, a Eurocentrist" (ibid., 124).

The challenge Dubois faced, and which marked him as non-Afrocentric, was largely a philosophical one that concerns three major ideological positions, namely, négritude, authenticity, and Afrocentricity. Asante states that of the three, Afrocentricity is the most powerful and comprehensive ideological-cum-existential stance against the enduring problematic of black identities and cultural replication:

> Afrocentricity is the most complete philosophical totalization of the African being- at-the-center of his or her existence. It is not merely an artistic or literary movement. Not only is it an individual or collective quest for authenticity, but it is above all the total use of method to effect psychological, political, social, cultural, and economic change. The Afrocentric idea is beyond decolonizing the mind. (ibid., 125)

The Afrocentric project seeks nothing short of the complete retrieval of the obscured African heritage, even when within the present it is forced to articulate a rhetoric of resistance filtered through an alien language. Black rhetoric has always sat uncomfortably with white America and even with African-Americans. Consequently, there is a discernible "attempt to keep the lid on the explosive discourse that lurks just below the surface of any public discussion of human rights" (ibid., 147).

Asante goes on to argue that the Western rhetorical tradition has been impoverished since Platonic times, when sophistry and the Sophists were denounced as being unphilosophical. Philosophical practice, according to the example of Plato, entailed a withdrawal from social interaction and a retreat into the realm of pure contemplation. This led to what Asante says was a "bifurcation of reality" and which "had the disastrous impact of denying the "arts of appearance" any legitimate connection to genuine thought and placed Greek thought against wholistic thought" (ibid., 137). Here, there is a convergence between Nabudere's ideas and those of Asante.

Nabudere claims that ancient Greek thought created and enforced a dialectical tradition of thought that prevented a holistic apprehension of reality. Asante posits that the Hellenic appearance versus reality conundrum truncated reality and, therefore, the possibilities of apprehending it in a wholesome manner. In his view, this bifurcation of the ontological lens did not occur in ancient Egypt, which upheld an integrated system of perception.

A myth – as well as statement of intent – that frequently crops up in African-American rhetoric and culture is the one concerning the return to Africa away from the bondage and oppression of America. Asante claims – but a contrary view exists – that Marcus Garvey is regarded as a fiery as well eloquent spokesman of this movement. According to this myth, Africa, the motherland, is perceived as a place of "unity, security, and liberty" (ibid., 155); it is held high as metaphor for deliverance and salvation, one in which the political actualization of the dream of liberation was a distinct possibility. It is also a myth that retains considerable Afrocentric interest.

Another major Afrocentric project is the invention of a genre of literary theory that would concentrate on Afrocentric aspects of literary production as distinct from the hegemonic Eurocentric tradition which is often touted as universal. An Afrocentric literary theory would aim at freeing words from the bias and constraints of the Eurocentric heritage. On a theoretical level, there is much for Afrocentricity to accomplish as it seeks to articulate forms of knowledge beyond the limits of Eurocentric epistemology with rationality, objectivity, and progress as its central precepts. In addition, positivism and empiricism as intellectual approaches within social science do not factor "the emotions, attitudes, and cultural definitions of a given context" (ibid., 164) and yet attempt to stand for totalization and universalism. On the other hand, Afrocentricity centralizes the importance of:

the interrelationship of knowledge with cosmology, society, religion, medicine, and tradition stands alongside the interactive metaphors of discourse as principal means of achieving a measure of knowledge about experience" (ibid.).

Rather than intellectual fragmentation, Afrocentric thought seeks wholeness, again another convergence with the ideas of Nabudere: It is also considered "the rationalization of the alternative consciousness." (ibid., 165) And then Asante stresses why Afrocentric theory is a necessity:

> African Americans who participate only in Eurocentric views can easily become anti-black, the logical extension of European cultural imperialism. To be sure, there have been a host of African American critics and theorists who have added to African literature and orature; however, too many still see themselves as serving some artificial value to European scholarship. They are victims of their own identity crisis, a crisis produced purely by their submission to the roles whites have forced them to play (ibid.).

Asante also mentions that Africa "is the seat of the oldest organized civilizations as well as the birthplace of humanity" a frequently routed credo of Afrocentric discourse and other related ideologies of blackness (ibid., 166) He reiterates the chronic identity crisis that bedevils blacks, which he expects to grow worse under worsening economic conditions. The crisis usually manifests in the form of "whited-out blacks who have fallen into the I-want-whites-to-accept-me trap, and even if they say "Accept me as I am," they mean "as I become whiter" (ibid., 167).

In order to overcome the absolute dominance of Eurocentric theory, the mere concentration on a few key motifs of Afrocentric discourse would not be enough. What is required is "an architectonic treatment, a total reclamation of philosophical ground" (ibid.). The reclamation of philosophical ground is made considerably more difficult because "much so-called black discourse is essentially white or Eurocentric discourse by black people" (ibid., 169). Blacks often find themselves in a position that grants support to prejudices and assumptions that negate their cultural and historical specificity. They engage in self-negation without often times being aware of it. And then Asante makes a proclamation that captures the spirit and essence of Afrocentricity:

> A truly Afrocentric rhetoric must oppose the negation in Western culture; it is combative, antagonistic, and wholly committed to the propagation of a more humanistic vision of the world. Its foundation is necessarily the slave narrative. Its rhythms are harmonious, discordant only to those who have refused to accept either the truth of themselves or the possibility of other frames of reference. Afrocentric rhetoric, while it is in opposition to the negative in Western culture, allows other cultures to co-exist, and in that particular aspect is substantially different from Western rhetoric. It is neither imperialistic nor oppressive. Therein lies its invigorating power (ibid., 170).

Afrocentric discourse also does not possess the either/or dichotomy that characterizes Western thought. Instead, Afrocentric thought processes, rather than encapsulating binarization, are marked by circularity; this is thought to be a major distinction between the two traditions. The circularity associated with the Afrocentric conception of knowledge is not of the purposeless variety, as innate within it is a striving toward completeness and wholeness and toward the establishment of balance and harmony. For Asante, the issues of balance and harmony are quite significant, as within the Afrocentric paradigm, how authors should be judged depends on the extent to which they are able to deploy their artistry in seeking and establishing harmony in the quest to communicate.

A particular quality that distinguishes African-American life and spirit is the depth of pathos to be found in the culture. Asante argues that pathos in the culture is so ingrained as to distinguish the African-American from say a Malian or Kenyan. The pathos is said to stem from the innumerable indignities of slavery and captivity, which create distinctive cadences and accents within the whole range of African-American forms of cultural expression.

Asante asserts that the same pathos can be found in varying degrees amongst blacks in Cuba, Jamaica, Brazil, Colombia, Barbados, Haiti, and Trinidad, all of whom have experienced devastation, tribulation, and redemption through slavery. It could be added that the pathos Asante detects in all these various black cultures is also present in South Africa, which also had a prolonged and brutal experience of racial oppression.

The presence and quality of pathos are, perhaps, the ultimate triumph of the black spirit in the midst of absolute negativity; by a curious quirk of destiny, an utterly negative collective experience and an abject stretch of history metamorphosed into almost ineffable and subliminal cadences. Not even the oppressive dispensation could have anticipated this dimension of triumph, which would go on to distinguish its former victims in a quite singular manner with a spirit, a history, a morality, and a culture not experienced by any other. The irony is that a much oppressed people employing African traditions of spirituality, in their incessant striving to gain liberty, ultimately broke onto vast creative horizons upon which to celebrate the very freedom that they sought through an incomparable mushrooming of potent cultural forms that now serve as a beacon for the rest of humanity.

By extension, culturally sensitive approaches need to be developed when studying black cultures because Eurocentric presuppositions are likely to fail or be unrepresentative. Furthermore, neo-Aristotelian, phenomenological, structuralist, logical positivist, and post-structuralist approaches to black culture, in Asante's view, are not expected to succeed. An approach more likely to succeed would be the establishment of the primacy of the spoken word, the use of spirituality, and the call-and-response practice prevalent in black cultures. So prevalent are these characteristic features that it is not difficult to discern a conceptual commonality between a preacher and an itinerant jazz musician. What also joins them culturally is "the perfect transcendent declaration, the generative, productive nommo, finally and emphatically made real" (ibid., 182).

Asante's claim regarding the Afrocentric origins of civilization is worthy of mention; it provides a sharp contrast to virtually all Eurocentric accounts:

> Human civilization began in the Nile Valley with the gifts of Nubia. The temples of Karnak and Luxor held secrets of the mysteries, which have been explored by Schwaller de Lubicz, Ben-Jochannan, Budge, Diop and others in great detail. The ancient mysteries contained in the books of the great priests of the holy lodges held the key to African transcendence nearly five thousand years before the Arab jihads swept out of Arabia and conquered Northern Africa, stamping out, for the most part, the indigenous Egyptian language and establishing Islam as religion and Arabic as language. The subsequent dispersal of secret societies to various other places on the African continent made it possible for the re-emergence of these secrets in the Yoruba Ifa, the Shona Mbira, and the Asante Okyeame system, among other traditions (ibid., 182).

This thesis above could not be more different to, for example, the Pelagasian hypothesis. I include it here to reiterate that competing theories about the origins of human civilization exist, and this one is particularly relevant because it stresses an Afrocentric viewpoint.

In addition, within the Afrocentric paradigm, the striving for transcendence is quite significant. It is a trait to be perceived in the black cultures of Brazil, Jamaica, Cuba, Haiti, and the United States, of which "Samba, Sango, Candomble, Santeira, Voodoo, Macumba, Umbanda, and Mial" (ibid., 183). Traditions of orality are notable avenues for seeking transcendence, spirituality, and sublimation. In attaining these states, the quest to establish cosmic harmony is central; "the African American view of a wholistic personality, which is the healthy person, is grounded in the African idea of *sudicism,* the spiritual commitment to an ideological view of harmony" (185). Although Asante does not use the term, the South African concept of "ubuntu" plays a crucial role in the establishment of universal harmony. Asante writes, "one person becomes human only in the midst of others. The person is defined as human by his or her actions that lead to harmony" (ibid.).

Indeed, the theme of realizing one's essence through interactions and communion with others, that is, discovering and recovering oneself through communion with others, is quite familiar in Afrocentric notions of humanity. Constantly re-activating one's self through interactions with others stands in sharp contrast with the vulgar ultra-individualist's dictum, "hell is other people," but within the Afrocentric paradigm it (communion with others) serves as the basis for accessing and granting life. Thus as Asante says:

> The African finds energy and life in the midst of persons; he or she does not escape
> to mountains, or the valleys, or the seashores in order to find energy. There is no
> "great tradition" of withdrawal in the African or African American tradition; ours
> is preeminently a tradition of remarkable encountering with others. (ibid., 187)

The notion of nommo is constitutive of both life and energy and it is what generates the striving for transcendence and harmony.

Afrocentricity, just as Afrikology, seeks to restore universal equilibrium destroyed by multiple forms of violence. Afrocentricity, in its humanistic and progressive persuasion, has nothing to do with anti-white racism perpetrated by some blacks. Instead, there is a nurturing philosophy behind it; a belief and expectation of redemption to re-establish natural harmony.

Eurocentrism does comprehend Afrocentricity as discourse and consciousness, and hence, it is unable to identify with the brutal history of racial denigration and slavery. This particular history produced a peculiar cultural and existential matrix that would forever remain singular by virtue of its extremity and exceptionalism. Many who stand outside the circle of this highly transformative experience and matrix invariably miss the point when attempting to represent it.

The strength of Afrocentric discourse lies in its powerful and convincing critiques of Eurocentrism and its multiple ways of construing its dominance. Some view the effort to establish the supremacy of ancient African cultures over the rest of humankind as being a gesture ridden with reverse Eurocentric intent and violence, and thus, less convincing. Nonetheless, as mentioned earlier, the critique of Eurocentrism is vital. The endeavor to establish the singularity and importance of the African historical experience as the means by which a re-orientation with the present, on the one hand, and a re-alignment with precolonial African systems of knowledge, on the other, via the Afrocentric prism can succeed, is to create a sense of continuity in African life. Afrocentricity, in this light, is therapy for the injured consciousness and seeks to transcend the injustice and iniquities of the African existential condition. It therefore has more than one major component; it is theory, history, and culture aligned with therapy and activism; it encompasses as a whole a set of well-aimed responses to the past, present and future survival. It centers on the regeneration of an entire race.

7

Conclusion: Before Afrocentricity

Asante has employed the concept of Africology in a way that sheds some light on it. In an interview published in *The Journal of Pan African Studies*, he had said:

> The most significant contributions of Africology (note the spelling is slightly different from Nabudere's) is that it has impacted all of the social sciences in ways that have changed them forever. It is because of us that sociologists do not speak the language of deprivation, disadvantaged, and minority in their best literature. It is because of that historians are willing to see black lives as critically important to a full understanding of the American society. They do not use the terms Bushman, Hottentots, pygmies, tribes, and primitives, as much as they used to before 1980. In effect, we have changed the language of the social sciences and reinvented the discourse around African people. We have become agents in our own history (2008: 81).

Africology also espouses a pan-African mandate in seeking to rebuild and revitalize African communities wherever in the world they are to be found. A scholar of Africology is not merely interested in careerism and public intellectualism. The agenda is far broader and deeper than those two usual preoccupations of academics, as it compasses the quest to transform society. More than that, it centers on the survival of a race.

Dani Nabudere's work in many ways intersects with Asante's definition of Africology. Nabudere had conducted early empirical studies on the ravages of imperialism in Africa. These studies bear a strong anti-colonialist element and are quite engaging. They have no "metaphysical" preoccupations with Afrikology, in the sense that they deal with the stark, brutalizing onslaught of imperial power in Africa. Even when the sociopolitical situation on the African continent appears to be marked by widespread despondency and seems destined to complete ruination, Nabudere's engagement with the realities is marked by an unflinching robustness that demonstrates that all hope is not lost. Just as the continent is abundantly endowed with impressive natural resources, so is his belief in the African cause truly inspiring.

Undoubtedly, Nabudere is a bold and engaging scholar. He took on the Ugandan leader, Yoweri Museveni, blaming him for much of the conflict occurring in the Great Lakes region. Such a stance is never a safe one to adopt, especially in contexts ruled by brutal despots and regimes. Here, Nabudere displays his métier as a committed activist rather than an ivory tower-based scholar.

Nabudere's account of the Great Lakes Region conflict clearly demonstrates the importance of Africa to him. The region itself can be described as all that is wrong with Africa, in which the chancre of virulent ethnicity wreaks untold havoc on often defenseless civilian populations; enormous mineral wealth rather than generating much-needed economic advancement becomes the harbinger of severe societal conflagration; the collision of powerful local and international interests undermining the entire nation-building project in the name of personal and corporate greed; the deployment of war as the principle through which fervently competing factions are precariously held in check; the normalization of death as a means of controlling already thoroughly brutalized subjects.

Nabudere's scholarship straddles two main currents, both of which display commitment to African development. The first, which characterizes his mid-life preoccupations, focus on current affairs, in which primary data collection approaches are prominent and little theoretical reflection is involved. The second current of Nabudere's scholarship explores the ramifications of the concept of Afrikology, which is largely theoretical and often disengaged from immediate African political concerns. This current also displays a marked preoccupation with spirituality or at least a pronounced humanism. The question might be posed: Could this be as a result of Nabudere's disenchantment with the contemporary political world?

Nabudere's analysis of the conflict situation in the Great Lakes region is highly perceptive. It is easy to focus on the rebel and militia-ridden ethnic strife, identity crises, and misguided and ambitious political opportunists who unleash violence on poor and hapless villages located amid fields of diamonds and gold. But Nabudere points to a much broader picture involving all kinds of international cartels working within and beyond the bounds of legality, all colluding in various bewildering combinations to loot the mineral wealth of the region.

Within the second major current in his thought, Nabudere argues that Afrikology advances a new philosophy based on African oral cultures, which in a way, is similar to Kwasi Wiredu's project of conceptual decolonization, a project concerned with combining indigenous epistemic retrieval and the gains of modernization (1995). However he also differs from Wiredu via an outright repudiation of Cartesianism.

Nabudere's project is commendable for its well-intentioned Afrocentricity, but faces an almost insurmountable conceptual aporia: How does one overcome the ineffability of the divine? How does one develop a vocabulary that embodies and truly describes a spirituality for which there is as yet no language? How does one traverse the enormous divide between mind and body, employing a language capable of encompassing both entities? The problem lies essentially with the limits of language, which is perennially entangled within the modalities of the body, to the apparently permanent exclusion of the mind or spirit. The language that can best describe the spirit, which Nabudere so much values, is at least submerged if not lost, perhaps to prehistory and possibly could only be excavated at the margins of cultures, which also face the problem of translating undervalued idioms across a divide that is insufferably opaque by virtue of the fact that they belong to a different order of conception.

Nabudere's approach to biblical sources is curious. He often debunks them in favor of prehistoric accounts and then reverts back to them whenever it suits him; hence, a glaring inconsistency is evident. According to his usage, Afrikology is transformed into an all-encompassing epistemology able to transcend the perceived fallacy and shortcomings of Cartesianism, able to engender true justice in social relations, able to act as an emancipatory program for oppressed peoples, and finally, able to restore the injured dignity of the black race. Afrikology, he claims, is able to accomplish all these aims and even more.

But in ascribing these attributes to Afrikology, in seeking a wholeness in both material and metaphysical terms, the grounds on which it is supposed to be based become fairly unstable. If it is truly able to accomplish all that is ascribed to it and more, then what really is it? Oftentimes it appears that Afrikology is just a word, a hint of a prescriptive program yet to be realized.

The exploration of indigenous knowledge systems (IKS) in epistemological terms is very similar to the contestations between orality and scribal culture in which IKS (understood here as part of orality) and science suspiciously view the modalities of each other. For IKS to be fully legible and appreciated, it has to be formulated and clearly expressed within the material texture and modes of enunciation of contemporary knowledge forms; it has to find a way to surmount this divide or face squarely the unsavory prospect of extinction.

Nabudere's privileging of the heart as the foundation of knowledge is obviously similar to the Senghorian négritudist assertion that rhythm is central to the African body and mind just as rationalism is a distinctive Western hallmark. In a way, Nabudere recasts négritude as Afrikology even when he engages European philosophers such as Gadamer and Habermas. Afrikology must be infused with a forthright rigor in order to meet the category of intellectual challenges posed by the Eurocentric intellectual tradition.

Nabudere's scholarship often acts as a bridge between ancient and contemporary knowledge, in which the former is construed as the more wholesome form. Contemporary knowledge, in Nabudere's view, is severely mutilated by its dialectical character and heritage. However, he does indicate how to traverse the divide between the two forms – the dialectic and holistic thought – that, when approached through a modern lens, are inextricably interwoven. The divide between the two that Nabudere stresses appears to be, in fact, a seamless evolution spanning the entire gamut of human thought.

Nabudere's espousal of transdisciplinarity is heavily based on the Western academic tradition, which he appears only too pleased to reveal at every turn by his copious references to Western authors and intellectual traditions. Sometimes, his advocacy of transdisciplinarity sits uneasily with his shifting notions of Afrikology. Transdisciplinarity bears strong hints of academic neutrality, while Afrikology often displays a marked racial agenda on the side of blackness. In this manner, transdisciplinarity conflicts with Afrikology, as both possess highly different antecedents and orientations as well as highly divergent aspirations. In addition, in proposing Afrikology, hermeneutics, and transdisciplinarity as the new modes of knowledge generation, Nabudere's project adopts the same kind of posture and intent as the universalists of science that he opposes. At this juncture, his proposition smacks of philosophical totalitarianism even when, in instances, he advocates the plurality of knowledge forms.

Nabudere claims that the Western form of the dialectic is the causal origin of all contemporary intellectual problems. But the dialectic itself, emerged as a result of the introduction of the triadic format of an epistemic system that paved the way for Nabudere's own discourse. The entire modern world as it is known is based on paradigmatic innovations – the writing culture, protoscience, the modern economy, and organized religion – which emerged as a result of progressive evolutions of the triadic system. Therefore, Nabudere's account of the dialectic as the primal source of intellectual confusion is more misleading than it is useful. In order to prove otherwise, he would have to present the intellectual gains of humankind before the institution of the triadic structure and then replicate those gains within the context of contemporary thought.

Nabudere's privileging of the heart as the source of all genuine knowledge is first and foremost an essentializing gesture that is, in fact, even more controversial than the worst excesses of négritude. The only way to give credibility to this thesis would be to conduct a series of epistemological exercises displaying products of the heart as the foundation of knowledge. In other words, a wealth of empirical data is necessary so as not to leave his thesis as what it would always be if not supported by solid evidence: an untested and unsubstantiated proposition. Unfortunately, there is as yet no language able to capture the full knowledge and spirit of the Nabuderean conception of the heart.

It is necessary to read Nabudere against Diop and similar thinkers because they are related to the discourse of Afrocentricity and its multiple aspirations. Also, both Nabudere and Diop employ similar ways to assert the primacy of black civilization. But the similarities end there.

Diop conducts extensive research on precolonial black Africa, which on its own is a quite impressive accomplishment. Nabudere ventures into a transdisciplinary discourse informed and constructed by the very Western dialectical traditions he fervently contests. Here lies not only a conceptual inconsistency, but also perhaps an anomaly. Indeed, Nabudere's Afrikology is quite similar to Diop's Egyptology, but with much less ethnographic evidence.

On the other hand, many Eurocentric attempts to accommodate Afrocentricity miss the spirit and intent of it. Afrocentricity as advanced by Asante is distinguished by two important features: the centrality and memory of the slave and the attitudes, responses, and pathos they generate, which permeate and inform virtually all aspects of African-American existence; this grants Afrocentricity its enduring relevance and its inviolability.

Within the traditional African context, holism features prominently in cosmological interactions and in interpretations of the universe; holism may appear in the form of the perception of medicine being linked to religion, agriculture, nature, and the village. This view is to be found in Nabudere's work in different propositions but with the same conceptual intent. Furthermore, his employment of Basarab Nicolescu, and even Cheikh Anta Diop, to advance his argument is often problematic. The conception of transdisciplinarity he applies is drawn from Cartesianism, which at the same time he refutes as the cause of the deleterious dichotomization of human knowledge.

Nabudere has obviously not discovered a vocabulary constituted outside of Cartesianism. Neither has he found a vocabulary that springs directly from the epicenter of African metaphysics. Accordingly, his entire project flounders between a Cartesianism it has not managed to shake off, and a notion of African metaphysics it has not succeeded to properly articulate. In addition, he fails to take into account that the mechanisms, practices, and institutions for knowledge generation have all been deeply transformed during the course of human development. It is also possible that significant genetic mutation has occurred from between the period of ancient Egypt and present times. Nabudere provides no indication as to how to transcend these radical transformations and developments in order to arrive at, and re-incorporate most of the ancient Egyptian heritage.

There is a fervent contestation throughout Nabudere's work between mind and body, between holistic thought and the dialectic, together with all its implications within the human intellectual tradition. Nabudere's subjectivity aligns him with the primacy of spirit over matter even as the language he is compelled to employ to state his case denounces spirit in unambiguous ways. The metaphysician who opposes the dialectic is forced to employ it as a philosophical conduit through which to attempt to privilege spirit over matter, thereby sometimes securing preposterous results in the process.

The dialectic possesses its own infinity but it is one completely captured, wedded to physicality, with no shade of metaphysics even when the notion of infinity is   essentially metaphysical; this creates a paradox that defies resolution, a paradox able to generate its own highly independent, godless universe, and capable of yielding a form of transcendence that is completely devoid of spirit. This is the ultimate cosmic disappointment, for which there could never be an appropriate existential response.

The infinity of the dialectic is one of the body as opposed to the spirit. One can only but wonder and 'utter what an outcome.' But the body is supposed to have no infinity, as it is defined at all events, by limits which hamper it inch by inch and moment by moment until it succumbs and disappears. It would appear that the dialectic in discovering infinity has rediscovered God all but in name; a universal deity devoid of metaphysics, religion or an afterlife because life itself has merged with the afterlife and annihilated the demarcation that was held in place by metaphysical sensibilities and conditions. In other words, God makes a re-appearance in a non-metaphysical world without the accompanying mythology and ceremony; a silent, desolate entrance that is akin to an unbearable nightmare and instead of bearing fire, warmth and comfort, He brings instead the cold ashes of desolation and unending wordless despair. There are curses upon curses without the regeneration and healing warmth of the word.

The dialectic having gotten rid of God, religion, and metaphysics institutes a process for itself that is no different from the effects of a deity; it is condemned to replicate itself within the expanse of infinity until it loses all traces of itself. Reason which had replaced God is found wanting and delimiting partly because its origins are suspect and partly because it frequently suffers from unreasonable spasms and interludes of malfunction. And so reason recedes while the dialectic devoid of origins or a master succumbs to nothingness which bears only the faintest intimations of its past. Nothingness too is marked by a listless unremittingness and being stripped and empty of spirit, loiters without purpose or meaning. This is the scenario that undoubtedly prompted Dani Nabudere's final reflections.

References

al-Sadi, Abd., 1898/1964, *Tarikh es-Soudan* [The history of the Sudan]. Edited and translated by O. V. Houdas and E. Benoist. Paris: Adrien-Maisonneuve. (French translation from Arabic)

Amin, Samir., 1989, *Eurocentricism*. London: Verso.

Asante, M. K., 1987, *The Afrocentric Idea*. Philadelphia, PA: Temple University Press. Asante, M. K., 1990, *Kemet, Afrocentricity, and Knowledge*. Trenton, NJ: Africa World Press. Asante, M. K., 1990, *Kemet, Afrocentricity, and Knowledge*. Trenton, NJ: Africa World Press.

Asante, M. K. and Itibari M. Zulu., 1987, "Africology 101: An Interview with Scholar Activist Molefi Kete Asante," *The Journal of Pan African Studies* 2, no. 2 (March): 79–84. http:// www.jpanafrican.com/docs/vol2no2/Africology101.pdf.

Bernal, Martin Gardiner., 1987–2006, *Black Athena*. 3 vol. New Brunswick, NJ: Rutgers Universty Press.

Carruthers, P., and A. Chamberlain, eds., 2000, *Evolution and the Human Mind: Modularity, Language and Meta-Cognition*. New York: Cambridge University Press.

Chenqu, Gerikai., 2014, "Before Columbus: How Africans Brought Civilization to America." Global Research Newsletter. http://tinyurl.com/onsaxy8.

Chomsky, Noam., 1986, *Knowledge of Language: Its Nature, Origin, and Use*. New York: Praeger.

Curtin, Philip D., 1981, "Recent Trends in African Historiography and Their Contribution to History in General." In *Methodology and African Prehistory*. Vol. 1 of *General History of Africa*. Edited by Jacqueline Ki-Zerbo. Berkeley: University of California Press.

Diop, C. A., 1974., *The African Origin of Civilization: Myth or Reality*. New York: L. Hill.

Diop, C. A., 1987, *Precolonial Black Africa: A Comparative Study of the Political and Social Systems of Europe and Black Africa, from Antiquity to the Formation of Modern States*. Westport, CT: Lawrence Hill Books.

Diop, C. A., 1991. *Civilization or Barbarism: An Authentic Anthropology*. Edited by H. J. Salemson and M. de Jager. Translated by Y.-L. M. Ngemi. Brooklyn, NY: Lawrence Hill. Du Bois, W. E. B., 2008, *The Souls of Black Folk*. New York: Oxford University Press.

Du Bois, W. E. B., 1976, *The World and Africa*. New York: Kraus-Thompson Organization.

Durkheim, E., 1965, *The Elementary Forms of Religious Life*. New York, Free Press. (Original French, 1912)

Durkheim, E., and M. Mauss., 1970, *Primitive Classification*. 2nd ed. Translated with an introduction by R. Needham. London: Cohen & West.

Empedocles., 1908, *The Fragments of Empedocles Translated into English Verse by William Ellery Leonard.* London &Chicago: Open Court.

Fairbanks, Arthur., 1898, *The First Philosophers of Greece.* London: Kegan Paul, Trench, & Trubner.

Fairman, H W., 1935, "The Myth of Horus at Edfu, I," *Journal of Egyptian Archaeology* 21: 26–36.

Fairman, H W., 1965, "Ancient Egypt and Africa," in "Proceedings of the 1964 Conference," special issue, *African Studies Association of the United Kingdom* 64: 69–75.

Falconer, Thomas, ed. and trans., 1797, *The Voyage of Hanno: Translated, and Accompanied with the Greek text: Explained from the Accounts of Modern Travellers, Defended against the Objections of Mr Dodwell, and Other Writers, and Illustrated by Maps from Ptolemy, d 'Anville, and Bougainville.* London: Cadell.

Fabian, Johannes., 1983, *Time and the Other: How Anthropology Makes Its Object.* New York: Columbia University Press.

Farnell, L. R., 1977, *The Cults of the Greek States.* New Rochelle, NY: Clarendon Press; original 1896.

Farnell, L. R., 1921, *Greek Hero Cults and Ideas of Immortality: The Gifford Lectures Delivered in the University of St. Andrews in the Year 1920.* Oxford: Clarendon.

Flemming, Harold C., 1987, "Proto-Gongan Consonant Phonemes: Stage One." in *Leo Reinisch, Werk und Erbe.* Edited by Hans G. Mukarovsky, 141–159. Wien: Verl. d Österreich. Akad. d. Wiss.

Flemming, Harold C., 1991, "A New Taxonomic Hypothesis: Borean or Boralean," *Mother Tongue: Journal of the Association for the Study of language in Prehistory* 14, Newsletter, ASLIP.

Gadamer, Hans-Georg, and Richard E. Palmer, 2007, The Gadamer Reader: A Bouquet of the Later Writings. Evanston, IL: Northwestern University Press.

Gates, Henry Louis, Jr., 1988, *The Signifying Monkey: A Theory of African-American Literary Criticism.* New York: Oxford University Press.

Griaule, Marcel., 1965, *Conversations with Ogotemmêli: An introduction to Dogon religious ideas.* Translated by R. Butler and A. Richards. New York: Oxford University Press for International African Institute.

Hoschchild, Adam., 1997, "Mr. Kurtz, I Presume," *The New Yorker*, April 4, 40.

Hountondji, Paulin., 2002, *The Struggle for Meaning: Reflections on Philosophy, Culture, and Democracy in Africa.* Athens: Ohio University Press.

Ibn Khaldûn., 1980, *The Muqaddimah: An Introduction to History.* 3 vol. 2nd ed. Translated by F. Rosenthal. Princeton, NJ: Princeton University Press; original Arabic c. 1377.

Jaspers, Karl., 2011, *The Origin and Goal of History.* Translated by Michael Bullock. London: Routledge.

Jung, C. G., 1974, Foreword to *The I Ching or Book of Changes.* 3rd ed. Translated by R. Wilhelm and C. F. Baynes. Princeton, NJ: Princeton University Press.

Kahler-Meyer, Emmi., 1988, "Myth Motifs in Flood Stories from the Grasslands of Cameroon." In *The Flood Myth.* Edited by A. Dundes, 249–59. Berkeley: University of California Press.

Kahn, C. H., 1960, *Anaximander and the Origins of Greek Cosmogony.* New York: Columbia University Press.

Kaiser, M., and V. Shevoroshkin, 1988, "Nostratic," *Annual Review of Anthropology* 17: 309– 29.

Kakar, S., 1983, *Shamans, Mystics and Doctors: A Psychological Inquiry into India and Its Healing Traditions.* Boston: Beacon Press.

Kaliff, Anders., 2007, *Fire, Water, Heaven and Earth: Ritual Practice and Cosmology in Ancient Scandinavia: An Indo-European Perspective.* Stockholm: Riksantikvarieambetet och Statens.

Kammerzell, F., 1994, *Panther Loewe und Sprachentwicklung im Neolithikum* [Panther Loewe and anguage development in Neolithikum]. Göttingen: Lingua Aegyptia Studia Monographica.

Kant, I. 1964. *Critique of Pure Reason.* Translated by N. Kemp Smith. London: Macmillan.

Keightley, David N., 1978, *Sources of Shang History: The Oracle-Bone Inscriptions of Bronze Age China.* Berkeley: University of California Press.

Keightley, David N., and N. Barnard, eds., 1983, *The Origins of Chinese Civilization.* Berkeley: University of California Press.

Keita, S. O. Y., 1993, "Black Athena: 'Race,' Bernal, and Snowdon," *Arethusa* 26: 295–314.

Kelsen, Hans., 1988, "The Principle of Retribution in the Flood and Catastrophe Myths." In *The Flood Myth.* Edited by A. Dundes, 125–49. Berkeley: University of California Press; original 1943.

Kemp, Barry J., 2007, *Ancient Egypt: Anatomy of a Civilisation.* London: Routledge.

Kent, R., 1970, *Early Kingdoms in Madagascar 1500–1700.* New York: Holt, Rinehart & Winston.

Kimambo, Isaria N., and A. J. Temu., 1969, *A History of Tanzania.* Evanston, IL: Northwestern University Press.

Kingsford, A. B., and E. Maitland., 1885, *The Virgin of the World of Hermes Mercurius Trismegistus.* London: George Redway.

Kingsley, Peter., 1994a, "Empedocles and His Interpreters: The Four-Element Doxography," *Phronesis* 39: 235–54.

Kingsley, Peter., 1994b, "From Pythagoras to the Turba Philosophorum: Egypt and Pythagorean Tradition," *Journal of the Warburg and Courtauld Institutes* 57: 316–24.

Kingsley, Peter., 1994c, "Greeks, Shamans, and Magi," *Studia Iranica* 23,187–98.

Kingsley, Peter., 1995a, *Ancient Philosophy, Mystery, and Magic: Empedocles and Pythagorean tradition.* Oxford: Clarendon.

Kingsley, Peter., 1995b, "Meetings with Magi: Iranian Themes among the Greeks, from Xanthus of Lydia to Plato's Academy," *Journal of the Royal Asiatic Society* 5: 173–209.

Kingsley, Peter., 1999, *In the Dark Places of Wisdom.* Inverness: Golden Sufi.

Kingsley, Peter., 2003, *Reality.* Inverness: Golden Sufi.

Kirchenhoffer, H., 1988, *Napoleon's Book of Fate: Ancient Egyptian Fortune-Telling for Today.* Edited by B. Parker. Wellingborough, Northamptonshire: Aquarian Press/New York: Distributed by Sterling.

Kirk, G. S., J. E. Raven, and M. Schofield., 1983, *The Presocratic Philosophers: A Critical History.* 2nd ed. Cambridge: Cambridge University Press.

Kirkbride, D., 1966, "Five Seasons at the Pre-Pottery Neolithic Village of Beidha in Jordan," *Palestine Exploration Quarterly* 98, no. 1 (Jan.–June): 8–72.

Kitz, Anne Marie., 1997, "The Plurald Form of 'Ûrîm and Tummîm," *Journal of Biblical Literature* 116, no. 3: 401–10.

Knecht, H., A. Pike-Tay, and R. White, eds., 1993, *Before Lascaux: The Complex Record of the Early Upper Paleolithic*. Ann Arbor: CRC Press.

Kovacs, M. G., 1985, *The Epic of Gilgamesh*. Stanford, CA: Stanford University Press.

Kramer, S. N., 1959, *History Begins at Sumer: Twenty-Seven "Firsts" in Man's Recorded History*. Garden City, NY: Doubleday.

Kroeber, A. L., 1940, "Stimulus Diffusion," *American Anthropologis*, 42, no. 1: 1–20.

Kunz, Hans., 1957, "Critique of Jaspers' Concept of 'transcendence,'" In *The Philosophy of Karl Jaspers*. Edited by P. A. Schilpp, 499–522. New York: Tudor.

Kyong-McClain, J., 2010, "Barbarian Caves or Han Tombs? Republican-Era Archaeology and the Reassertion of Han Presence in Ancient Sichuan," *Twentieth Century China* 35, no. 2: 4–24.

Laks, André., 2005, "Some Thoughts about Empedoclean Cosmic and Demonic Cycles and the Byzantine Anonymous." In Pierris, *The Empedoclean Kosmos*, 265–282.

Lambert, W. G. 1975. "The Cosmology of Sumer and Babylon." In *Ancient cosmologies*. Edited by C. Blacker and M. Loewe, 42–65. London: Routledge & Kegan Paul.

Lambridis, Helle., 1976, *Empedocles: A Philosophical Investigation*. Tuscaloosa, AL: University of Alabama Press.

Lambropoulou, Voula., 1998, "The Concept of Harmony in Greek Thought from Homer to Aristotle: 3, Cosmology," *Platon* 50: 145–68.

Lange, Dierk., 2004, *Ancient Kingdoms of West Africa: Africa-Centred and Canaanite- Israelite Perspectives: A Collection of Published and Unpublished Studies in English and French*. Dettelbach: Röll.

Lange, Dierk., 2009, "An Assyrian Successor State in West Africa: The Ancestral Kings of Kebbi as Ancient Near Eastern Rulers," *Anthropos* 104, no. 209: 359–82.

Lanning, Greg, and Marti Mueller., 1979, *Africa Undermined: Mining Companies and the Underdevelopment of Africa*. New York: Penguin.

Layton, R. 2001. "Shamanism, Totemism and Rock Art: *Les Chamanes de la Prehistoire* [The shamans of prehistory] in the Context of Rock Art Research," *Cambridge Archaeological Journal* 10: 169–86.

Lefkowitz, Mary R., 1994, "The Myth of a 'Stolen Legacy,'" *Society* 31, no. 3: 27–33.

Lefkowitz, Mary R, and G. MacLean Rogers, eds., 1996, *Black Athena Revisited*. Chapel Hill: University of North Carolina Press.

Legge, James, trans. 1882. *The Sacred Books of China. The Texts of Confucianism. Pt. 2, The Yi King*. Oxford: Clarendon Press.

Legge, James, trans. and ed., 1993, *I Ching /Book of Changes*. The Chinese-English Biliigual Series of Chinese Classics. Beijing: Hunan Publishing House.

Leibniz, Gottfried Wilhelm., 1994, *Writing on China*. Edited and translated by Daniel J. Cook and Henry Rosemont Jr. LaSalle, IL: Open Court.

Leibold, J., 2011, "Filling in the Nation: The Spatial Trajectory of Prehistoric Archaeology in Twentieth-Century China." In *Making History Modern: Constructing the Discipline in China*. Edited by B. Moloughney and P. Zarrow, Peter. Hong Kong: Chinese University Press.

Levtzion, N., and J. F. P. Hopkins, eds., 1981, *Corpus of Early Arabic Sources for West African History*. New York: Cambridge University Press.

Lévy-Bruhl, L., 1923, *Primitive Mentality*. New York: Macmillan.

Levy, G. R., 1934, "The Oriental Origin of Herakles," *Journal of Hellenic Studies* 54: 40–53, and Plate ii.

Lewis-Williams, J. D., 2002, *The Mind in the Cave: Consciousness and the Origins of Art.* London: Thames & Hudson.

Lewis-Williams, J. D, and T. A. Dowson., 1988, "The Signs of All Times: Entoptic Phenomena in Upper Palaeolithic Art," *Current Anthropology* 29: 201–45.

Li Fan., 2005, "Between Nationalism and International Identity: Analyze the Hypothesis of Chinese Civilization West Coming of Liu Shipei," *Historiography Quarterly* 4.

Li, X., G. Harbottle, J. Zhang, and C. Wang, C., 2003, "The Earliest Writing? Sign Use in the Seventh Millennium BC at Jiahu, Henan Province, China," *Antiquity* 77: 31–44.

Liddell, H. G., and R. Scott. 1901. *A Greek-English Lexicon.* Oxford: Clarendon.

Lieu, S. N. C., 1994, *Manichaeism in Mesopotamia and the Roman East.* Leiden: Brill.

Linton, R., 1933, *The Tanala: A Hill Tribe of Madagascar.* Anthropological Series 22. Chicago: Field Museum of Natural History.

Lloyd, G. E. R., 1964, "The Hot and the Cold, the Dry and the Wet in Greek Philosophy," *Journal of Hellenic Studies* 84: 92–106.

Long, A. A., 1974, "Empedocles' Cosmic Cycle in the Sixties." In *The Pre-Socratics: A Collection of Critical Essays.* Edited by A. P. D. Mourelatos, 397–425. Garden City: Anchor/ Doubleday Press.

Longrigg, James., 1963, "Philosophy and Medicine: Some Early Interactions," *Harvard Studies in Classical Philology* 67: 147–75.

Longrigg, James., 1967, "Roots," *Classical Review* 17: 1–4.

Longrigg, James., 1976, "The 'Roots of All Things,'" *Isis* 67: 420–38.

Lucas, Jonathan Olumide., 1948, *The Religion of the Yorubas, Being an Account of the Religious Beliefs and Practices of the Yoruba peoples of Southern Nigeria, Especially in Relation to the Religion of Ancient Egypt.* Lagos, Nigeria: C.M.S. Bookshop.

Malthus, Thomas R., 1798, *An Essay on the Principle of Population as it affects the Future Improvement of Society with Remarks on the Speculations of Mr. Godwin, M. Condercet and Others.* London: Printed for J. Johnson.

Mamdani, M., 2001, *When Victims Become Killers: Colonialism, Nativism, and the Genocide in Rwanda.* Princeton, NJ: Princeton University Press.

Mudimbe, V. Y., 1988, *The Invention of Africa: Gnosis, Philosophy, and the Order of Knowledge.* Bloomington: Indiana University Press.

Nabudere, D. Wadada., 1980, *Imperialism and Revolution in Uganda.* Onyx Press: London.

Nabudere, D. Wadada.,1994, "The African Challenge," *Alternatives: Global, Local, Political* 19, no. 2 (Spring):163–71.

Nabudere, D. Wadada., 1997, "Beyond Modernization and Development, Or, Why the Poor Reject Development," *Geografista Annaler: Series B, Human Geography* 79, no. 4: 203–15.

Nabudere, D. Wadada., 2002, "How New Information Technologies Can be Used for Learning in Pastoral Communities in Africa" World Social Summit, Porto Alegre, Brazil. http://tinyurl.com/ pjaq2ko.

Nabudere, D. Wadada., 2003, "Conflict Over Mineral Wealth: Understanding the Second Invasion of the DRC." In *The War Economy in the Democratic Republic of Congo.* Edited by S. Naidoo. Braamfontein, South Africa: Institute of Global Dialogue.

Nabudere, D. Wadada., 2004, "Traditional and Modern Political Systems in Contemporary Governance in Africa," *Journal of African Elections* 3, no. 1: 13–41.

Nabudere, D. Wadada., 2006, "Towards an Afrokology of Knowledge Production and African Regeneration," *International Journal of African Renaissance Studies* 1, no. 1: 7–32.

Nabudere, D. Wadada., 2004, "Africa's First World War: Mineral Wealth, Conflicts, and War in the Great Lakes Region." Pretoria, South Africa: African Association of Political Science.

Nabudere, D. Wadada., 2011, *Afrikology, Philosophy, and Wholeness: An Epistemology.* Pretoria: Africa Institute for South Africa.

Nabudere, D. Wadada., 2012, *Afrikology and Transdisciplinarity: A Restorative Epistemology.* Pretoria: Africa Institute for South Africa.

Oppenheim, A. L., 1966, "Perspectives on Mesopotamian Divination." In *La divination en Mesopotamie ancienne et dans les régions voisines* (Divination in ancient Mesopotamia and neighboring regions). *XIVe Rencontres Assyriologiques Internationale, Strasbourg, 2-6 juillet 1965* (14th International Assyriological Dating Conference, Strasbourg, 2–6 July 1965). Edited by Centre d'Études Supérieures Spécialisé d'Histoire des Religions de Strasbourg. Paris: Presses Universitaires de France.

Oppenheimer, Stephen., 2001, *Eden in the East: The Drowned Continent of Southeast Asia.* 2nd ed. London: Weidenfeld and Nicolson.

Rashidi, R., 1988, "Diminutive Africoids. First People of the Philippines." In African Presence in Early Asia. Edited by I. van Sertima and R. Rashidi, 354–59. New Brunswick, NJ: Transaction.

Robb, John E., 1998, "The Archaeology of Symbols," *Annual Review of Anthropology* 27, no. l: 329–46.

Robbins, L. H., and A. C. Campbell., 1990, "Prehistory of Mungongo Nut Exploitation in the Western Kalahari Desert, Botswana," *Botswana Notes & Records* 22: 37–39.

Robertson, Edward., 1961, "Urim and Thummim," In vol. 22 of *Encyclopaedia Brittanica: A New Survey of Universal Knowledge.* Edited by H. S. Ashmore, 897. Chicago: Encyclopaedia Britannica.

Robinson, K. R., 1959, *Khami ruins: Report on Excavations undertaken for the Commission for the Preservation of Natural and Historical Monuments and Relics, Southern Rhodesia, 1947– 1955.* New York: Cambridge University Press.

Rochberg, Francesca., 2002, "A Consideration of Babylonian Astronomy within the His-toriography of Science," *Studies in History and Philosophy of Science* 33, no. 4: 661–84.

Rodney, Walter., 1974, *How Europe Underdeveloped Africa.* Nairobi, Kampala, and Dar es Salaam: East African Educational Publishers.

Rollefson, G. O., 1992, "A Neolithic Game Board from 'Ain Ghazal, Jordan," *Bulletin of the American Schools of Oriental Research* 286 (May): 1–5.

Ronnberg, A., and Ginneken, C. van., 2011, eds, *Het boek der symbolen* [The book of symbols]. Köln: Taschen.

Rose, H. J., 1935, "'Nvmen Inest': 'Animism' in Greek and Roman Religion," *The Harvard Theological Review* 28, no. 4: 237–57.

Rostomev, M. I., 1929, *The Animal Style in South Russia and China.* Princeton, NJ: Princeton University Press.

Rowley, H. H., 1956, *The faith of Israel: Aspects of Old Testament Thought.* London: Students Christian Mission Press.

Ruhlen, Merritt., 1998, "The Origin of the Na-Dene," *Proceedings of the National Academy of Sciences of the United States of America* 95: 13,994–6.

Runciman, S., 1969, *The Medieval Manichee: A Study of the Christian Dualist Heresy*. Cambridge: Cambridge University Press; original 1947.

Rutt, Richard., 2002, *The Book of Changes (Zhouyi): A Bronze Age Document*. New York/London: Routledge.

Sagart, Laurent., 1999, *The Roots of Old Chinese*. Amsterdam: Benjamins.

Said, E. W., 1979, *Orientalism*. London: New York: Random House, Vintage Books.

Sapir, E., 1913, "A Girls' Puberty Ceremony among the Nootka Indians," *Transactions of the Royal Society of Canada*, 3rd Series 7: 67–80.

Schapera, I., 1952, *The Ethnic Composition of Tswana Tribes*. London: London School of Economics and Political Science, Monographs on Social Anthropology, 11.

Scheub, Harold., 2000, *A Dictionary of African Mythology: The Mythmaker as Story Teller*. New York/Oxford: Oxford University Press.

Schmandt-Besserat, D., 1992, *Before Writing: From Counting to Cuneiform. I.* Austin: University of Texas Press.

Schmidt, P., 1933, "Persian Dualism in the Far East." In *Oriental Studies in Honour of Cursetji Erachji Pavry*. Edited by J. D. C. Pavry, 405–6. Oxford: Oxford University Press.

Schoff, Wilfied H., ed. & trans., 1913, *The Periplus of Hanno: A Voyage of Discovery Down the West African Coast by a Carthaginian Admiral of the Fifth Century B. C.* Philadelphia: Commercial Museum.

Simon, David., 2012, "Remembering Dani Wadada Nabudere," *Review of African Political Economy* 39, no.132: 343–4.

Simonse, S., 1992, Kings of Disaster: Dualism, Centralism and the Scapegoat King in Southeastern Sudan. Leiden: Brill.

Simonse, S., 1980, *Terrestial Astrology: Divination by Geomancy*. London: Routledge & Kegan Paul.

Smith, Brian K., 1991, "Classifying Animals and Humans in Ancient India," *Man*, New Series 26, no. 3: 527–48.

Smith, Brian K., 1994, *Classifying the Universe: The Ancient Indian Varna System and the Origins of Caste*. New York/Oxford: Oxford University Press.

Smith, E. W., and Dale, A. M., 1920, *The Ila-Speaking Peoples of Northern Rhodesia, I- II.* London: Mamillan.

Smith, G. Elliot., 1919, *The Evolution of the Dragon*. Manchester: Manchester University Press/ London, New York: Longmans, Green & Company.

Smith, G. Elliot.,1929, *The Migrations of Early Culture: A Study of the Significance of the Geographical Distribution of the Practice of Mummification as Evidence of the Migration of Peoples and the spread of Certain Customs and Beliefs*. 2nd ed. Manchester: Manchester University Press; original 1915.

Smith, R. J., 2012, "How the *Book of Changes* Arrived in the West," *New England Review*, 33, no. 1: 25–41.

Smith, William, ed., 1880, *A Dictionary of Greek and Roman Biography and Mythology, I-II.* London: Murray.

Snow, P., 1988, *The Star Raft: China's Encounter with Africa*. London: Weidenfeld & Nicolson. Snowdon, F. M. S., Jr. 1970. *Blacks in Antiquity: Ethiopians in the Graeco-Roman Experience*. Cambridge, MA: Harvard University Press.

Snow, P., 1989, "Bernal's 'Blacks,' Herodotus, and Other Classical Evidence," in "The Challenge of Black Athena," eds. M. M. Levine, M. Myerowitz, and J. Peradotto, special issue, *Arethusa*, 22, l: 83–95.

Soderblom, L. A., and T. V. Johnson., 1982, "The Moons of Saturn," *Scientific American* 246: 101–14.

Soetens, Katinka., 2008, "The Source Goddess of the Chauvet Caves," *Goddess Alive!: Goddess Celebration and Research* 14 (Autumn/Winter). http://www.goddess alive.co.uk/index. php/issues-11-15/issue-14/chauvet.

Solheim, W. G. I., II., 2000, "Taiwan, Coastal South China and Northern Viet Nam and the Nusantao Maritime Trading Network," *Journal of East Asian Archaeology* 2, no. 1–2: 273–84.

Solmsen, F., 1965, "Love and Strife in Empedocles' Cosmology," *Phronesis* 10: 123–45.

Sophocles. 1993. *Complete Works*. Vol. II: *Ajax, Electra, Trichiniae, Philoctetes*. Translated by F. Storr. Cambridge, MA: Harvard University Press.

Sorenson J. L., and C. L. Johannessen., 2004, "Scientific Evidence for Pre-Columbian Transoceanic Voyages to and from the America," *Sino-Platonic Papers* 133 (April).

Sorenson, John L., and M. H. Raish., 1996, *Pre-Columbian Contact with the Americas across the Oceans, I-II*. 2nd ed. Provo, UT: Research Press.

Sparks, Rachael. 2006. "Acholi Wheel Trap," Southern Sudan Project, Pitt-Rivers Museum, accession number 1922.25.6, from Acholi, Sudan, collected by C.G. and B.Z. Seligman., 1922," http://tinyurl.com/omssl6t.

Sphujidhvaja., 1978, *The Yavanajataka of Sphujidhvaja*. Edited and translated from Sanskrit by D. E. Pingree. Cambridge, MA: Harvard University Press.

Spivak, G. C., 1987, *In Other Worlds: Essays in Cultural Politics*. London: Methuen.

———., 1990, *The Postcolonial Critic*. New York: Routledge.

Sprague, R. K., 1972, "Empedocles, Hera, and Cratylus, 404 c," *The Classical Review* NS 22, no. 2: 169.

Staal, F., C. V. Somayajipad, I. R. Nambudiri, and A. De Menil., 1984, *Agni: The Vedic Ritual of the Fire Altar*. Delhi: Motilal Banarsidass.

Stanley, G. A. V. 1926. "String-Figures of the North Queensland Aborigines. Part 1," *Queensland Geographical Journal* 1926: 73–92.

Starostin, Sergei A., 1989, "Nostratic and Sino-Caucasian." In *Exploration in Language Macrofamilies*. Edited by V. Shevoroshkin, 42–66. Bochum: Brockmeyer.

Starostin, Sergei A., 1991, "On the Hypothesis of a Genetic Connection between the Sino-Tibetan Languages and the Yeniseian and North-Caucasian Languages [Translation and Introduction by W. Baxter III]." In: *Dene-Sino-Caucasian Languages: Materials from the First International Interdisciplinary Symposium on Language and Prehistory. Ann Arbor, Michigan, November 1988*. Edited by V. Shevoroshkin, 12–41. Bochum: Brockmeyer.

Shingo, S., 1984, *A Study of the Toyota Production System from an Industrial Engineering Viewpoint*. Tokyo: Japan Management Association.

Soros, George., 1998, *The Crisis of Global Capitalism: Open Society Endangered*. New York: Public Affairs.

Rawls, John., 1971, *A Theory of Justice*. Cambridge, MA: Belknap Press of Harvard University Press.

Temple, R. F. G., 1976, *The Sirius Mystery*. London: Sidwick & Jackson.

Terrien de Lacouperie, A. E. J.-B., 1880, *Early History of the Chinese Civilization*. London: Vaton.

Terrien de Lacouperie, A. E. J.-B., 1887a, *Babylonia and China [Investigations into Their Ancient Affinities]* London: Babylonian and Oriental Record.

Terrien de Lacouperie, A. E. J.-B., 1887b, The Fabulous Fishermen of Early Babylonia in Ancient Chinese Legends. London: Babylonian & Oriental Record.

Terrien de Lacouperie, A. E. J.-B., 1888a, *The Old Numerals, the Counting Rods and the Swan-Pan in China*. Reprinted from the *Numismatic Chronicle* vol. 3 (1883): 297–340. http://babel.hathitrust.org/cgi/ pt?id=ucl.b5604122;view=1up;seq=3.

Terrien de Lacouperie, A. E. J.-B., 1888b, "The Origin of the Babylonian Characters from the Persian Gulf," *Journal of the Royal Asiatic Society of Great Britain and Ireland*, New Series 20 no. 2: 316–9.

Terrien de Lacouperie, A. E. J.-B., 1890, *The Onomastic Similarity of Nai Hwang-ti of China and Nakhunte of Susiana*. London: Nutt.

Terrien de Lacouperie, A. E. J.-B., 1892a, *The Loan of Chaldaeo-Elamite Culture to Early China*. London: Nutt.

Terrien de Lacouperie, A. E. J.-B., 1892b, *The Oldest Book of the Chinese: The Yh-king and Its Authors*. London: Nutt.

Terrien de Lacouperie, A. E. J.-B., 1894, *Western Origin of the Early Chinese Civilization from 2,300 B.C. to 200 A.D., or, Chapters on the Elements Derived from the Old Civilizations of West Asia in the Formation of the Ancient Chinese Culture*. London: Asher.

Terrien de Lacouperie, A. E. J.-B., 1897, *The Langauges of China before the Chinese: Researches on the Languages Spoken by the Pre-Chinese Races of China Proper Previously to the Chinese Occupation*. London: Nutt.

Tester, S. J., 1989, *A History of Western Astrology*. New York: Ballantine.

Thomas, P. V., J. D. Morrison, M. Davies, and T. V. Johnson., 1983, "Saturn's Small Satellites: Voyager Imaging Results," *Journal of Geophysical Research* 88, no. A11: 8743–54.

Thorndike, L., 1923–1958, *A History of Magic and Experimental Science: During the First Thirteen Centuries of Our Era, I-VIII*. New York: Columbia University Press.

Thornton, R., 2012., "Glass Beads and Bungoma: The Link between Southern India and Southern African Traditional Knowledge Known as Bungoma." Paper read at the International Conference on Rethinking Africa's Transcontinental Continuites in Pre- and Protohistory," African Studies Centre, Leiden, April12–13. http://tinyurl.com/p34mkkw.

Tibbets, G. R., 1971, *Arab Navigation in the Indian Ocean before the Coming of the Portuguese*. Oriental Translation Fund, New Series vol. 42. London: Royal Asiatic Society of Great Britain.

Usuanlele, Uyilawa, and Toyin Falola., 1994, "The Scholarship of Jacob Egharevba of Benin," *History in Africa* 21: 303–318. Stable URL http://www.jstor.org/stable/3171890?origin=JSTOR-pdf.

Van Beek, W. E. A., 1991, "Dogon Restudied: A Field Evaluation of the Work of Marcel Griaule," *Current Anthropology* 32, no. 2: 139–67.

Van Binsbergen, Wim M. J., 1995, "Divination and Board-Games: Exploring the Links between Geomantic Divination and Mancala Board-Games in Africa and Asia." Paper read at the 1995 International Colloquium on Board-Games in Academia, Leiden, April 9–13; published as "Rethinking Africa's Contribution to Global Cultural History: Lessons from a Comparative Historical Analysis of Mancala Board-Games and Geomantic Divination," special issue, Tatlana: *Proceedings of the Dutch Archaeological and Historical Society* 29: 221– 54; revised version at http://www.shikanda.net/ancient_models/gen3/mankala.html.

Van Binsbergen, Wim M. J., 2008, "Transcontinental mythological patterns in prehistory: A multivariate contents analysis of flood myths worldwide challenges Oppenheimer's claim that the core mythologies of the Ancient Near East and the Bible originate from early Holocene South East Asia," *Cosmos: The Journal of the Traditional Cosmology Society*, 23: 29–80.

Van Binsbergen, Wim M. J., 2011a, "Existential Dilemmas of a North Atlantic Anthropologist in the Production of Relevant Africanist Knowledge." In *The Postcolonial Turn: Re- Imagining Anthropology and Africa*. Edited by René Devisch and Francis B. Nyamnjoh, 117–42. Bamenda, Cameroon: Langaa/Leiden:/African Studies Centre.

Van Binsbergen, Wim M. J., 2011b, "Is There a Future for Afrocentrism Despite Stephen Howe's Dismissive 1998 Study?" In Van Binsbergen, ed. *Black Athena Comes of Age*, 253–82.

Van Binsbergen, Wim M. J., 2011c, "The Limits of the Black Athena Thesis and of Afrocentricity as Empirical Explanatory Models: The *Borean Hypothesis, the Back-into- Africa Hypothesis and the Pelasgian Hypothesis as Suggestive of a Common, West Asian Origin for the Continuities between Ancient Egypt and the Aegean, with aNew Identity for the Goddess Athena." In Van Binsbergen, ed. *Black Athena Comes of Age*, 297–338.

Van Binsbergen, Wim M. J., 2011f, "Matthew Schoffeleers on Malawian Suitor Stories: A Perspective from Comparative Mythology," in "A Tribute to the Life of Fr. Matthew Schoffeleers (1928–2011): Malawianist, Renaissance Man and Free-Thinker," eds. Louis Nthenda and Lupeaga Mphande, special memorial edition, *The Society of Malawi Journal* 64, no. 3: 6–94.

Van Binsbergen, Wim M. J., 2011d, "Shimmerings of the Rainbow Serpent: Towards the Interpretation of Crosshatching Motifs in Palaeolithic Art: Comparative Mythological and Archaeoastronomical Explorations Inspired by the Incised Blombos Red Ochre Block, South Africa, 70 ka BP, and Nkoya Female Puberty Rites, 20th c.CE." http:// shikanda. net/ancient_models/crosshatching_FINAL.pdf

Van Binsbergen, Wim M. J., 2012, *Before the Presocratics. Cyclicity, Transformation, and Element Cosmology: The Case of Transcontinental Pre- or Protohistoric Cosmological Substrates Linking Africa, Eurasia, and North America*. Leiden: African Studies Centre. *This volume has an excellent bibliography of other works by Wim van Binsbergen regarding this and related topics.

Van Binsbergen, Wim M. J., 2012b, "A Note on the Oppenheimer-Tauchmann Thesis on Extensive South and South East Asian Demographic and Cultural Impact on Sub-Saharan Affica in Pre- and Protohistory." Paper read at the International Conference on Rethinking Africa's Transcontinental Continuities in Pre- and Protohistory," Afirican Studies Centre, Leiden, April 12–13. http://tinyurl.com/pszl8tt.

Van Binsbergen, Wim M. J., 2012c, "Production, Class Formation, and the Penetration of Capitalism in the Kaoma Rural District, Zambia, 1800–1978." In *Lives in Motion, Indeed: Interdisciplinary Perspectives on Social Change in Honour of Danielle de Lame*. Edited by Cristiana Panella, 223–72. Studies in Social Sciences and Humanities 174. Tervuren: Royal Museum for Central Africa.

Van Binsbergen, Wim M. J., 2012d, "The Relevance of Buddhism and Hinduism for the Study of Asian-African Transcontinental Continuities." Paper read at the International Conference on Rethinking Africa's Transcontinental Continuities in Pre- and Protohistory," African Studies Centre, Leiden, April 12–13. http://www. shikanda.net/ topicalities/Mwendanjangula_final.pdf.

Van Binsbergen, Wim M. J., 2012e, "Rethinking Africa's Transcontinental Continuities in Pre- and Protohistory." Keynote paper read at the International Conference on Rethinking Africa's Transcontinental Continuities in Pre- and Protohistory." African Studies Centre, Leiden, April 12–13. http://tinyurl.com/oyzb98n.

Van Binsbergen, Wim M. J., 2012f., "Towards a Pre- and Proto-Historic Transcontinental Maritime Network: Africa's Pre-Modern Chinese Connections in the Light of a Critical Assessment of Gavin Menzies' Work. http://tinyurl.com/oq2hpo8.

Van Binsbergen, Wim M. J., 2013, "African Divination Across Time and Space: Typology and Intercultural Epistemology." In *Realities Revealed. Divination in sub-Saharan Africa*. Edited by Walter E. A. van Beek and Philip Peek, 339–75. Berlin:Munster/Boston: LIT.

Vansina, Jan., 1985, *Oral Tradition as History*. Madison: University of Wisconsin Press.

Vasunia, Phiroze. 2001. *The Gift of the Nile: Hellenizing Egypt from Aeschylus to Alexander*. Berkeley: University of California Press.

Vico, Giambattista., 1968, *The New Science of Giambattista Vico*. Revised translation of the 3d ed. (1774) Thomas Goddard Bergin and Max Harold Fisch. Ithaca, NY: Cornell University Press.

Wainwright, G. A., 1940, "192. The Egyptian Origin of the New Year's Sacrifice at Zanzibar," *Man* 40: 164–7.

Wainwright, G. A., 1949, "Pharaonic Survivals, Lake Chad to the West Coast," *Journal of Egyptian Archaeology* 35: 167–75.

Wainwright, G. A., 1951, "231. The Egyptian Origin of a Ram-Headed Breastplate from Lagos," *Man* 51: 133–5.

Waite, A. E., ed., 1893, *The Hermetic Museum, Restored and Enlarged; Most Faithfully Instructing All Disciples of the Sopho-Spagyric Art How That Greatest and Truest Medicine of the Philosopher's Stone May Be Found and Held. Now First Done into English from the Latin Original Published at Frankfort in the year 1678; Containing Twenty-Two Most Celebrated Chemical Tracts*. London: Elliott.

Walker, D. P., 1972, *The Ancient Theology*. Ithaca, NY: Cornell University Press.

Walters, D., 1992, "The Way of the Emperor: The Oracle and Game of Mah Jongg." In *The World Atlas of Divination: The Systems: Where They Originate: How They Work*. Edited by J. Matthews, 128–35. Boston: Little Brown.

Wang Feng., 2005, "On the Genetic Position of the Bai Language," *Cahiers de Linguistique-Asie Orientale* 34, no. 34–1:101–27. http://tinyurl.com/pk8du6o.

Warrington Eastlake, F., 1880, "Chaldean Grammamancy," *China Review* 9: 120–2.

Watts, I,. 2009, "Red Ochre, Body Painting, and Language: Interpreting the Blombos Ochre." In *The Cradle of Language*. Edited by R. Botha and C. Knight, 62–92. Oxford: Oxford University Press.

Weeks, Mary Elvira., 2003, *Discovery of the Elements*. Whitefish, MT: Kessinger; original 1935.

Weiner, Leo., 1920, *Africa and the Discovery of America*, vol. 2. Philadelphia, PA: Innes and Sons.

Werbner, R. P., 1989, "Making the Hidden Seen: Tswapong Wisdom Divination." In *Ritual Passage Sacred Journey: The Process and Organization of Religious Movement*. Edited by R. P.

Werbner., 1960. Washington, D.C.: Smithsonian Institution Press.

Werner, E. T. C., 1984, *Myths and Legends of China*. Singapore: Singapore National Printers Ltd; original 1922.

Wescott, R. W., 1961, "Ancient Egypt and Modern Africa," review of *The Religion of the Yoruba in Relation to the Religion of Ancient Egypt*, by Olumide Lucas, *The Journal of African History*, 2, 2: 311–21.

West, M. L., 1971, *Early Greek Philosophy and the Orient*. Oxford: Clarendon.

West, M. L., 1983, *The Orphic Poems*. Oxford: Oxford University Press.

West, S. 1988. "The Scythian Ultimatum (Herodotus IV 131, 132)," *Journal of Hellenic Studies* 108: 207–11.

Whitehead, A. N., 1997, *Science and the Modern World: Lowell Lectures, 1925*. New York: Free Press.

Widengren, G., 1965, *Mani and Manichaeism*. London: Weidenfeld & Nicholson.

Wiens, H. J., 1949, "The Shu Tao or Road to Szechwan," *Geographical Review* 39, no. 4: 584–604.

Wilcox, J., 2001, "'Whole-Natured Forms' in Empedocles' Cosmic Cycle." In *Essays in Ancient Greek Philosophy VI: Before Plato*. Edited by A. Preus, 109–22. Albany: State University of New York Press.

Wilensky, J., 2002, "The Magical Kunlun and "Devil Slaves": Chinese Perceptions of Dark-Skinned People and Africa before 1500," *Sino-Platonic Papers* 122.

Wilkinson, T. A. H., 2001, *Early Dynastic Egypt*. London/New York: Routledge.

Winters, Clyde A., 1980, "A Note on the Unity of Black Civilizations in Africa, Indo-China, and China." In *PISAS 1979*. Hong Kong: Asian Research Service.

Willis, Roy, ed., 1993, *World Mythology*. London/New York: Duncan Baird. Wilson, M. 1957. "140. Joking Relationships in Central Africa," *Man*: 111–2.

Winters, Clyde-Ahmad., 1981a, "Are Dravidians of African Origin," *Proceedings Second International Symposium on Asian Studies, 1980*. Hong Kong: Asian Research Service, pp. 789–807.

Winters, Clyde-Ahmad., 1981b, "Further Thoughts on Japanese Dravidian Connection," *Dravidian Language Association News* 5, no. 9: 1–4.

Winters, Clyde-Ahmad., 1981c, "The Unity of African and Indian Agriculture," *Journal of African Civilization* 3, no. 1: 103.

Winters, Clyde-Ahmad., 1983a, "The Blacks of China's First Civilization: The Xia," http://olmec98.net/xia.htm.

Winters, Clyde-Ahmad., 1983b, "Possible Relationship between the Manding and Japanese," Papers in Japanese Linguistics 9: 151–8.

Winters, Clyde-Ahmad., 1985a, "The Genetic Unity between the Dravidian, Elamite, Manding, and Sumerian Languages," Proceedings of the Sixth ISAS, 1984," Hong Kong: Asian Research Service, 1413–25.

Winters, Clyde-Ahmad., 1985b, "The Proto-Culture of the Dravidians, Manding Sumerians," *Tamil Civilization* 3, no. l: 1–9.

Winters, Clyde-Ahmad., 1988a, "The Dravidian and Manding Substratum in Tokharian," *Central Asiatic Journal* 32, no. l–2: 131–41.

Winters, Clyde-Ahmad., 1988b, "Tamil, Sumerian, Manding, and the Genetic Model," *International Journal of Dravidian Linguistics* 8, no. 1: 67–91.

Wiredu, K., 1995, *Conceptual Decolonization in African Philosophy*. Ibadan: Hope Publications.

Index

Lightning Source UK Ltd.
Milton Keynes UK
UKHW011118051219
354770UK00002B/323/P